Praise for
The Hedgewitch's Little Book of Flower Spells

"A beautifully written book by a witch who clearly knows her magick… A true treasury of knowledge with an abundance of spells that use such a wide array of flowers, it would be easy to adapt any spell to where you live. The analogy of the universe as a spiderweb has opened a whole new way of thinking for me that will stay with me as I make magick of my own. This is a wonderful gem of a book, a must for any green or hedgewitch, or anyone with an interest in natural magick."

—Donna Trinder, owner of Green Witch Lincs

"This enchanting spellbook will really sing to the hearts of nature lovers, herbalists, light workers, and Wicca folk. The magic in the spells, flower identification, and the blessings for our garden insects makes this gem an absolute must-have."

—Nicky Alan, psychic and medium,
author of *M.E. Myself and I: Diary of a Psychic*

"Tudorbeth has created another amazing book, full of history, lore, and all that flower power! As a hedgewitch and a gardener, I have loved each of her books, but I fell madly in love with this book. Tudorbeth is known for blessing each of her books with vast amounts of knowledge and simple spells for everyday witches. Whether you are looking for spells for love, success, or dealing with toxic individuals, there are spells in here for every witch! This book should be an addition to every witch's library!"

—Brittany "Pagan" Adkins, host of
Pagan's Witchy Corner podcast

THE
Hedgewitch's
LITTLE BOOK OF
Flower Spells

© Sarah Coyne

ABOUT THE AUTHOR

Tudorbeth is the principal of the British College of Witchcraft and Wizardry and teaches courses on witchcraft. She is the author of numerous books, including *A Spellbook for the Seasons* (Eddison Books, 2019). Tudorbeth is a hereditary practitioner; her great grandmother was a well-known tea reader in Ireland while her Welsh great grandmother was a healer and wise woman.

THE
Hedgewitch's
LITTLE BOOK OF

Flower
Spells

TUDORBETH

Llewellyn Publications
Woodbury, MN

FIRST EDITION
First Printing, 2023

Book design by Donna Burch-Brown
Cover design by Shira Atakpu
Interior art by the Llewellyn Art Department

Llewellyn Publications is a registered trademark of Llewellyn Worldwide Ltd.

Library of Congress Cataloging-in-Publication Data (Pending)
ISBN: 978-0-7387-7140-3

Llewellyn Worldwide Ltd. does not participate in, endorse, or have any authority or responsibility concerning private business transactions between our authors and the public.

All mail addressed to the author is forwarded but the publisher cannot, unless specifically instructed by the author, give out an address or phone number.

Any internet references contained in this work are current at publication time, but the publisher cannot guarantee that a specific location will continue to be maintained. Please refer to the publisher's website for links to authors' websites and other sources.

Llewellyn Publications
A Division of Llewellyn Worldwide Ltd.
2143 Wooddale Drive
Woodbury, MN 55125-2989
www.llewellyn.com

Printed in China

Other Books by Tudorbeth

The Hedgewitch's Little Book of Spells, Charms & Brews

The Hedgewitch's Little Book of Seasonal Magic

Dedication

Dedicated to the rainbow and all who live within its varied colours; may we all be blessed with your beauty, truth, and grace.

Disclaimer

The material contained in this book is for information purposes only. It is not intended to be a medical guide or a manual for self-treatment. The information represented in this book is not a substitute for medical counselling or treatment prescribed by your doctor. It is not intended to diagnose, treat, or cure any diseases, mental health problems, or ailments.

This book is sold with the understanding that the publisher and author are not liable for the misconception, misinterpretation, or misuse of any information provided.

If you have a medical problem, please seek competent professional medical advice and assistance.

Contents

Contents

Introduction

Hedgewitchery is everywhere, and nowhere more so than in nature itself: in flowers, trees, herbs, and every form of flora imaginable. Every part of a plant can be used in magic, from the colour to the leaves to the stem and, finally, to the flower and petals themselves.

Hedgewitchery is that part of the Craft that is deeply esoteric, solitary, elemental, and totally "out there." I always describe it to fellow sisters and brothers, who follow the more traditional paths of witchcraft, as making the impractical, practical. We commune with elemental spirits, we travel the hedges, we live at the border, and we have one foot in this world and one in the other. Another thing about hedgewitches is that no two ever practice the same way as we recognise and respect individuality. The only part of witchcraft we recognise as the same are the correspondences, which are everything in the universe.

As a hereditary practitioner of the Craft, I was often told that the universe is a giant spider's web, and every strand is connected to another. When we use one part of that web, we are tugging on a strand, which in turn is pinging another, alerting the spider or the universe to what we want. Using correspondences, we are alerting the universe that we want something, and by connecting different correspondences, we are asking for attention. My family stemmed from Wales, Ireland, and Scotland and brought their knowledge of flowers and their power to each new generation. My father passed his knowledge onto me, having received that knowledge from his healer and midwife mother, Winifred, and his grandmother, Flora, who knew every plant and its purpose.

In this book, we shall look at one strand in that giant spider's web: we are looking at flowers and flora generally. This leads me to how this book is written. As this book will be worldwide, I am unsure of what flowers grow in your country. Therefore, the flowers are categorized by their colour. In the correspondences, certain strands shout louder than others, and colours are an enormously powerful correspondence. We will also categorize the colours by the rainbow, which in itself is an incredibly powerful strand within that giant spider's web. There are seven colours within the rainbow: red, orange, yellow, green, blue, indigo, and violet. Each colour governs other correspondences; for example, red represents love, sex, passion, action, and courage, to name but a few.

Furthermore, seven is one of the most magical numbers within our world. There are seven days of creation, seven days of the week, seven deadly sins, and seven virtues. There are the seven major chakra points of the human body and the seven-year itch. In folklore, it is said that a seventh son will be a werewolf. Other European folklores disagree, believing that the seventh son of a seventh son is always a magical, mystical child with great power for healing and clairvoyance. But still others say that the seventh son of a seventh son is a vampire. There are many connections within this sacred number and within the magical rainbow of colours.

Alongside the flower spells, there are also quotes and sayings stemming from ancestors. People who watched the turning of the year and could tell what the coming winter or season would bring just by looking at the behaviour of a flower. For example, *When the scarlet pimpernel closes, it's going to rain.* The scarlet pimpernel is a little flower that is often regarded as a weed in gardens, waste grounds, and dunes. It has many nicknames, including the poor man's weatherglass and shepherd's sundial.

A word of warning regarding flower magic: this form of magic cannot be used to change someone's will; therefore, you cannot make someone fall in love with you. If you try to influence another person, even for what seems to be a good reason, it becomes dark magic. Human beings have free will, people choose their paths, and we must never interfere with the decisions and choices people have made, no matter how much we want to. The spells contained in this book are light and full of love, but please use them wisely.

As we are all connected through the correspondences of this world, there are also the other life-forms that grace our plants and gardens, for without them, our flowers would die. Therefore, you will also find amongst these pages blessings for bees, birds, and creepy-crawlies. You will also find references to the gods and goddesses and other elementals who walk beside us in this garden of life we call the world.

In amongst the many flowers, there are also other forms of flora, such as herbs, blossoms of fruit trees, and certain spices that can be used in spells. Remember, everything in nature is connected, and that includes the world of flowers. Many herbs have flowers, as do many spices and their plants, the cinnamon flower being one example. There is so much colour and wonder everywhere in this world. Plants and flowers grow according to nature, and we can help them grow with love, care, and magic.

I hope you enjoy this book and casting its spells, and always cast with light and love in your heart. And above all, embrace the real flower power!

Blessed be.

The Bare Necessities

There are some essentials to flower magic that you need to be aware of before starting. The most important thing to remember is that flower magic should never harm the environment, including you. Therefore, please do not digest any flower you are unfamiliar with. Also, never pick wild-flowers as many of them are on the endangered species list for flora, and it's crucial that we leave them in their natural habitat. If you do come across a rare plant, photograph it and notify your local wildflower society; most countries have them now.

Furthermore, when performing a spell that calls for a flower you are unable to attain, use a photo instead. Focus your mind on the image of the flower instead of the actual plant.

Flower Parts & Parts Used

Flowers come in a variety of shapes, sizes, and colours, with different growing and flowering times. Despite the vast differences, they all have a similar structure. Flowers have both male and female parts, which enables them to reproduce. The male parts are called stamens and produce a fine dust-like substance called pollen. The female part is called ovules and produces the seeds.

My ancestors had different names for not only flowers, but also for the different parts, too. For example, the stamen was called the eye, and if a spell called for the eye of a peacock, it simply meant the stamen of an iris plant (we called iris flowers peacocks).

The petals surrounding these male and female parts attract insects so that the pollen can be transferred to other flowers. Therefore, attracting insects to the garden is paramount to the pollination and fertilization of flowers and plants. If you do not have insects in the garden, you will not have flowers!

And just as each part of the flower is used within nature, so it is within magic. From the flower to the stem, petals, stamen, seeds, bulbs, and roots, all can be used within magic.

Planting

When planting any flower, always follow the guidelines and make sure it is well watered and fed as required. Also, when buying a flower, think about its meaning and purpose in your garden. For example, is it a practical plant that will attract butterflies and bees into the garden, both of which are excellent pollinators? Or perhaps you are buying a plant to keep a certain species out, such as cats (but if you are a witch, good luck with that, as they will naturally be attracted to you and come to your garden). It is said that cats dislike the smell of rue, lavender, lemon thyme, and

Coleus canina—though I grow these plants in abundance and have many cats roaming my garden!

Also think about the colour scheme and effect you wish to create in your garden. Try to plant flowers that would grow naturally in your temperate zone and climate and always test the soil. For years, my mother wanted rhododendrons growing in the garden, but they never would as they need an acidic soil (they grow naturally in the Himalayas, Japan, and China). However, our soil is quite alkaline, so we planted them in pots with special acidic soil. To test the soil in your area, there are many pH garden scale kits you can buy at garden centres.

Drying

Just like herbs, flowers can be used fresh or dried. Get into the habit of drying certain flowers at their peak throughout the year and storing them in glass jars.

A particularly scarce flower to harvest throughout the year is the blossom as blossoms on various fruit trees only appear at certain times of the year. One of our most sacred blossoms is the hawthorn blossom, which is beautiful and gone within weeks. Harvesting and drying these blossoms is very important.

Drying flowers is a long process that requires patience, but it is worth it. This is a generic process you can use for any flowers, including blossoms from fruit trees, elderflowers, hawthorn, and chamomile flowers. This process is perfect for dying herbs, too.

Pick your flowers anytime between 6:00 a.m. and noon as this is when they are at their best. Discard any damaged or diseased material. Fill a bowl with cool water and add the fresh flowers. Gently clean the flowers, removing any insects, and sieve off debris that floats to the surface. Allow flowers to soak for a few minutes after cleaning. Remove the flowers and strain with a colander or salad spinner, ensuring that as much moisture as possible is removed. Paper towels may also be used as long as they do not disintegrate.

Heat an oven to 200 degrees Fahrenheit. While the oven is warming up, place the individual flowers on a baking tray lined with baking paper. Once the oven heats up, turn the oven off and place the baking tray on the lowest rack. Ensure that the oven door remains slightly

open and allow the flowers to dry. Check for dryness at regular intervals. If the flowers are not dry after a few hours, reheat the oven and begin the process again. Once the flowers are dry, place them in an airtight jar and store them for up to a year in a cool dry place.

Nature's Helpers

Flowers need bees, birds, butterflies, and all manner of insects to survive. We need these little helpers of nature for the health and longevity of flora within our world. And we need to show our gratitude to these wonderous little creatures. I was always taught to acknowledge these mighty little pollinators who grace our gardens and to show them the respect they deserve.

The following blessings and incantations are for nature's little helpers as without them, we would not have flowers, and if we don't have flowers, we won't have flower magic.

The Birds

When you awake at the first light of dawn, go outside or open your window and bless the birds. Say these words to the skies:

I hear your song
Your morning sweet call
Your evening lullaby
A gentle heavenly cry
Bless you little one
For the seasons you bring
The beauty of all you sing

You can also say this blessing as you put food out for the birds. It is always important to feed them, especially in winter, when nature's food is scarce.

The Bees

Welcome the bees to your garden by casting this spell. Plant some plants that bees love, such as lavender, rhododendron, and California lilac. As you plant your lavender for spring, your catmint for summer, your buddleias for autumn, and your hellebores for winter, say this spell to invite the bees into the garden. In the spring, walk around your garden, ideally in a circle, and recite this spell three times:

> *Welcome little bees*
> *To my garden*
> *Buzz here and there*
> *From flower to flower*
> *Do as you please*

Leave a little saucer of water for the bees in the summer—nothing too deep as you don't want to drown them.

The Butterfly

Buddleia is a shrub lovingly referred to as the butterfly bush. It is native to Asia, Africa, and the Americas, but it is now found all over the world as there are currently over one hundred forty varieties.

Buddleia can grow wild anywhere and everywhere and is a very hardy plant, often growing amongst paving stones and walls and other places that are difficult to access. Therefore, it is often regarded as an invasive, and many keen gardeners

will keep a close watch to make sure it does not take over. Nevertheless, it is a beautiful plant to have due to its popularity with both butterflies and bees.

Butterfly Dance Incantation

I sing this to the tune of "Lord of the Dance," but you can create your own rhythm to sing this incantation to. It needs to be something happy and upbeat.

On an early spring or summer morning, go into your garden and raise your hands to the sun. Say,

> *Blessed father, hear my call*
> *I embrace your gifts one and all*
> *Let the dance of your creatures great and small*
> *Enter now into my garden, hear my call*
> *Butterfly dance in gardens of many*
> *Delighting those you meet*
> *Spreading joy to those you greet*
> *Happy colours and silken wings*
> *Goddess blessings that you bring*

After you have finished, bow your head to nature and say thank you to your garden. Try to keep a record of how many butterflies come into the garden as their numbers are also dwindling, just like the bees. We all need to be aware of even the smallest changes in our planet's ecosystem. Many countries now have a nature watch organisation, so let them know how many butterflies you have seen.

The Spider

Folklore tells us, *If you want to live and thrive, let a spider run alive.* Yet so many people fear the spider; this fear is mostly unfounded. The majority of the world's spiders do not kill and bite humans on purpose. Indeed, many of the spiders we encounter do not kill at all and will certainly not bite. If anything, a spider encountering a human will run in the opposite direction.

In magic, the spider is our friend and ally. Indeed, many witches have a spider familiar, which is a guide and protector. We see the universe as a giant spider's web with everything connected on what is known as the correspondence web of life, and life for us is eternal.

Spider Fate Spell

Spiders represent good luck, prosperity, and good business transactions, so always let a spider run alive and never kill one. When you see a spider's web in your garden, say this spell over it if you are awaiting news. If cast upon a spider's web, the news will be positive.

> *I spin my web*
> *And cast my net*
> *Whatever I catch is my fate*
> *Patient forever I can wait*

Wait seven days for the news or the outcome. If you have not received anything after that time, cast the spell on a spider's web a second time, and wait another seven days. If you still have not heard anything after that, contact whomever you are waiting to hear from.

Ladybird

Many people know the old nursery rhyme of the ladybird (or ladybug as she is otherwise known in various places of the world). We look fondly on the ladybird; ladybirds are carnivores and are a bonus to have in any garden. They feed on aphids, greenflies, and other annoying insects that destroy plants. In the insect world, these little beetles that children all over the world love are quite maleficent. For this reason, we embrace the ladybirds and ask them to protect our gardens and plants from those insect pests that would harm our flowers.

Ladybird Invitation to the Garden Spell

If you haven't noticed ladybirds in your garden and insects are nibbling your roses, instead of reaching for the insecticide (not recommended), entice ladybirds into your garden. On a dry evening, stand barefoot in your garden and open your palms as though a ladybird was about to land on them. Say this spell:

> *Ladybird, ladybird, fly to my garden*
> *Eat the insects and protect all my flowers*
> *Please stay for many hours*
> *You are most welcome*

Stand for a few moments and imagine a ladybird flying onto your palms, then imagine putting it on the leaf of an infested plant. Often when I have performed this, an actual ladybird does appear; she might for you, too.

Flower Magic and Lore

Floriography is the language of flowers that became extremely popular in Britain during the Victorian era. Flowers were given high status and each flower had a meaning. Lovers would send secret coded bouquets to one another. For example, if someone sent six red roses, it meant they were infatuated with you; twelve red roses is a marriage proposal. The colour, the flower, and the number of flowers in a bouquet all held a meaning: red tulips are a symbol of a soul mate, white tulips are condolences or an apology, and so on.

The index at the back of this book lists many flowers and their meanings. Here are some general tips, notes, and correspondences that apply to flower magic to help you get started.

White Flower Warning

One word of caution regarding nature and flower magic. All white flowers belong to the Goddess, especially white lilac, white heather, elderflower, and pure, fragile hawthorn flowers in spring. These are sacred and must always be respected; therefore, when using these, please ask nature itself if you may cut a few flowers. On no occasion pick white heather or white lilac and bring them into the house as bad luck will follow—something I found out the hard way in my rebellious youth!

White & Black Flowers

White and black flowers have high magical importance and are used according to their meanings. Here is a chart on black and white flowers and their properties.

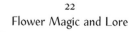

White Flowers	Meaning and Spell Intent
carnations	motherhood family protection spells
camellia	love and affection adoration spells
Japanese anemone	anticipation career and luck spells
gypsophila or baby's breath	everlasting love happiness spells
bouvardia	enthusiasm abundance spells
tulips	condolence forgiveness spells
orchids	innocence and elegance beauty spells
calla lily	overcoming challenges rebirth spells
snowdrops	purity home spells

Black Flowers	Meaning and Spell Intent
dahlia	diversity and unity teamwork spells
cosmos	tranquillity work-life balance spells
pansy	attracting love love spells
petunia	resentment and anger forgiveness spells
roses	hope new beginning spells
calla lily	resurrection faithfulness spells
queen of the night tulip	strength power spells
bat orchid	confidence communication spells
black magic hollyhock	fertility ambition spells

The Goddess

Traditionally, flower magic is ruled by the feminine and overseen by the pentacle of the Goddesses: five goddesses who represent the elements and all related correspondences, including flowers and plants.

Goddesses feature in some of these flower spells. There are also gods who are called to the different flowers based on their origin stories. If you do not follow the gods, omit the deity's name in any workings and in its place use the term *universe*.

Goddess	God	Direction	Colour	Flower
Gaia	Uranus	spirit	white	blossom
Iris	Hyacinthus	east	blue	lotus hyacinth
Diana	Priapus	west	green	moonflower zucchini flower
Morrigan	Narcissus	north	yellow	aconite jonquil
Aradia	Crocus	south	red	poppy crocus

Communication with Mystical Beings

In hedgewitchery, the belief in the elementals and mystical beings is central. The earth is full of energy we cannot see, such as gravity, air, and electricity. The beings of this energy are similar, though some people have been lucky to see them in all their splendour. The mystical beings are not only the Fae, but also nymphs, muses, angels, and dragons, to name a few.

Their energies align with the flower colour correspondences. They look after and care for the earth and nature, including us. Many a famous person has sought them out, including gardeners to help with their displays. Farmers have also been known to acknowledge the earth energies by offering food and wine and cider to the spirits of orchards to help future harvests. Some have called upon the muses and nymphs for inspiration and guidance in designing a garden or helping with a sickly plant.

In each chapter, there is a particular contact spell or ritual to invite elementals into your garden or home. Remember, we are connected to everything, and all in nature demands our respect. Please tread carefully in this world, and leave no litter anywhere. We are all gardeners in one way or another.

Correspondences

The correspondences are fundamental within hedgewitchery as they dictate how we cast spells, perform rituals, make brews, and generally live our lives. The correspondences are everything you see, feel, smell, taste, and believe in this world. They are the colours, the planets, the days of the week, the foods you eat, the sounds you hear, the feelings you have, and more.

Day: Sunday
Colour: orange and gold
Number: 1, 11
Month: January, October

Day: Monday
Colour: white and silver
Number: 2, 22
Month: February, November

Day: Tuesday
Colour: red
Number: 9
Month: September

Day: Wednesday
Colour: yellow
Number: 5
Month: May

Day: Thursday
Colour: blue
Number: 3, 7
Month: March, July

Day: Friday
Colour: green
Number: 6
Month: June, December

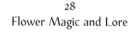

Day: Saturday
Colour: black
Number: 8, 4
Month: August, April

We are connected to everything on that giant spider's web via the correspondences, and every strand is one point of reference of life. Colours, plants, seasons, days of the week, flowers, feelings, emotions, careers—remember, the connections are endless. We learn these correspondences as witches, and learning them all takes many years.

Red Flower Spells

Love is the first thought when it comes to red flowers, and in magic it is no different. Red flowers and love go together like bees and summer; they are perfect companions. There are many variations of the theme of love, and flower spells can help with these. Spells for love, passion, romance, unrequited love, fertility, and more can be found within this area of magic.[1]

---

1. For more love spells and spells in general, please read *The Hedgewitch's Little Book of Spells, Charms & Brews* (Llewellyn Publications, 2021).

Red Correspondence Chart

Day: Tuesday

Gods: Mars, Lugh, Aradia

Physical: adrenal glands, kidneys, spinal column

Crystals: ruby, garnet, carnelian, red jade, red jasper, red sardonyx

Governs: love, sex, passion, action, romance, courage, physical energy, desire, power, will

The Flowers

Here is a selection of red flower spells to use along with the correspondences. Remember, if these flowers are not available where you live, use other red flowers or use a photo in place of the actual flower.

Azalea

Rhododendron

Keywords: Willpower, determination

There are over a thousand varieties of rhododendron found all over the world. It is the national flower of Nepal and the

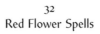

state flower of Washington and West Virginia in the United States of America. Certain rhododendron species have been used in traditional herbal medicine and made into tea. This tea is not recommended as the plant is highly toxic, with people becoming ill even by eating the honey made by bees harvesting on rhododendrons. Nevertheless, the red azalea is a perfect flower to use in a spell for enhancing will and determination during a difficult task.

Azalea Will Spell

Write out in a red pen the task or goal that is proving difficult. Try to use just one word. For example, if it is an essay or project for work, simply write *essay* or *project*. Have an azalea flower next to you (or a picture of one). Say this spell twice:

> *Will I may, will I might*
> *Boost my will to be forthright*

Roll up the flower in the paper and tie the paper with a piece of red ribbon or string. If you are using a picture of the flower, roll that in the paper, too. Leave the roll for two

weeks in a place where it will be undisturbed. When your task or project is complete, dispose of the flower and paper by burying them in the garden.

Camellia

Camellia japonica

Keywords: Desire, wish

The Japanese camellia is often referred to as the rose of winter, given that it can bloom during winter months. There are thousands of colour variants and flower forms of this plant as it is one of the most popular plants to cultivate. It is native to Japan and Asia, especially China, but it is now found all over the world. In China during Chinese New Year, the symbol of camellias is a sign of good luck and fortune.

The bright red camellia flower is a powerful plant to use in a desire spell. Desire can be for anything, not just for love. You can desire a career, a house, wealth, or even health. Desire is a powerful feeling as we yearn for something we want.

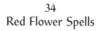

The Destiny Spell

This is a generic destiny spell. Think on three things you desire before performing it.

Have a photo of the Japanese camellia flower near you. Light a red candle and imagine what you would like your life to be. Say the spell into the candle three times:

> *Blessings to you, camellia flower*
> *Bring me* [insert your three desires]
> *Grant me all that I desire*
> *But be gentle with my life and tender with my fate*
> *In the past, present, and future, for glory I can wait*
> *Respect to nature for you grant me*
> *For now, and evermore, unfold camellia destiny*

Look at the photo of the camellia and imagine each petal unfolding wider. Within each petal is a desire you want. Blow out the candle and watch the rising smoke take your desires into the universe.

Cherry

Prunus avium

Keyword: Power

Certain tree flowers have wonderous strength and beauty. Cherry blossoms are one of the key ingredients in many love spells, and they are also used in fertility and friendship spells. The cherry fruit itself is highly prized due to its health benefits. Studies have shown that cherry juice can improve the duration and quality of sleep. Scientists have also discovered a direct relationship between the consumption of cherries and lowering fat levels in the body, particularly stubborn belly fat.

Cherry Power Sleep Juice Spell

If you want to feel powerful for a particular meeting or have an eventful day coming up and need to be at the top of your game, cast this spell. You will feel powerful and full of zest for your important day.

Ingredients

Half a glass of sugar-free cherry juice

1 tablespoon of aloe vera juice

Method

Mix the cherry juice and aloe vera. Add water and shake well before pouring into a warm glass. Enjoy. As you slowly sip your cherry juice, cast this spell, repeating it three times:

> *In this juice is the power*
> *Fruits of cherry flower*
> *Instil my sleep with rest*
> *I awake with power and zest*

Drink your juice and feel its red power flowing into you. Go to bed and have a good night's sleep. When you awake in the morning, you will feel powerful and exuberant.

Cuckoo's Eye

Geranium robertianum

Keywords: Willpower, strength

This plant, which grows wild in the hedgerows of Britain, has many different names, including herb Robert, red robin, stork's bill, crow's foot, cuckoo's eye, and even death-come-quickly or bloodwort. This lovely plant produces tiny pink flowers with five petals, which are perfect for practitioners

of the Craft who refer to it as the plant of magic. (Every plant with five petals will be associated with magic due to the connection with our sacred symbol, the pentagram.) Its stems and leaves can have red veins. Cuckoo's eye is regarded as a lucky plant, and people carry the flower with them to attract luck.

Cuckoo's eye is also a remedy for toothache and nose-bleeds. It can repel mosquitoes, so if you are camping, especially near lakes, and are being attacked by the midges, find this flower and rub some of the leaves on you. Cuckoo's eye can also be used as a gargle for sore throats and mouth ulcers; it is good for inflammations of the skin and for diarrhoea. Some also say this plant boosts the immune system and can help in the treatment of some cancers.

Extra Willpower Plant of Magic Spell

If your willpower is low but there are changes you want to make, cast this spell with this plant of magic. If you are lucky enough to have this wildflower growing in your garden, pluck a flower or two and recite this spell while holding the flowers.

Little flower of the wild
Grant me extra willpower
Let it run through all areas of my life
Little flowers boost my will and end my strife

Bury the little flower in the garden; the earth will receive your request. Go ahead with your newfound willpower and make those changes.

Dianthus

Dianthus caryophyllus
Keyword: Love

The dianthus is perhaps better known as carnations. This beautiful flower stemming from the Mediterranean has been cultivated for over two thousand years and signifies love the world over. Though it is not just red or pink that signifies love—the white carnation represents pure love and is best used for love that is young, new, and innocent.

Carnation Show Me the Love Spell

A red carnation is a wonderful symbol of love. If there is someone you have your eye on, send a little bunch of carnations to them. Use red, but if there are none available, use the pink variety. After you have ordered your dianthus, imagine the recipient receiving them, and say these words:

> *Show me the love that I show to you*
> *Carnation is sweet and so are you*
> *Please reciprocate so we become two*

Be patient and wait to see what happens. Your intended should contact you to thank you, and if they don't, wish them love and walk away, for they are not meant to be with you.

Dog Rose

Rosa canina
Keyword: Action

This beautiful flower, otherwise known as wild rose, can be found around the world. The pale pink flowers are perfect for spells and charms of love, especially romantic love. The rose hips that colour our hedgerows are full of vitamin C; for this reason, dog rose was planted all over the world. Its rose hips can be turned into teas, syrups, and marmalades. During World War II, it was planted in the Victory Gardens of the United States, which helped with food shortages during this turbulent time.

The War of Roses Spell

This flower is a saviour and a survivor, a perfect flower for battles not only in love but also in life. It is a flower of action and movement and getting yourself out of a rut. If you have been through a difficult time with a relationship and are finding it difficult to say goodbye, it is time for action and to move on. Only you can get yourself out of this negative place, so use the power of this delicate plant, which is so fierce and strong that it grows anywhere. This spell can be used not only for a love relationship but also for a friendship that has run its course, as this is a spell for saying goodbye. Pick a bunch of wild roses and bring them

into the house. Place a photo of your loved one or friend under the vase and say,

> *We've been through our wars*
> *We've fought and you brought me tears*
> *But now let us find peace*
> *For I still love thee*
> *My love renews and ends my fears*
> *I wish you nothing but the best throughout the years*

Keep the flowers in the vase for as long as possible with the photo underneath. When the flowers start to fade, throw them out immediately, giving thanks to the Goddess.

Geranium

Geranium

Keywords: Romance, love

The geranium is a staple plant in many gardens around the world, but the geranium is very revered in magic. The flowers have five petals, and any plant that has five leaves or flowers is a plant of magic given to us by the Goddess. We can use this plant for so many things in magic, but given its red colour, it is perfect for love and especially romance.

Send My Love to Me Spell

Buy a red geranium and keep it indoors or outdoors—whichever is best for the plant. Understand that this plant is a gift to the goddess Venus for helping you in your spell. Write the name of your beloved either in red or on red paper and fold the paper six times. Put the folded paper into the soil with the plant and say these words:

> *Venus and Mars, lovers of old*
> *Send my love to me, let love unfold*
> *This name I give to show thee*
> *This plant I give to you*
> *Let its flowers bloom with love*
> *As my love flourishes*
> *An' it harm none, so mote it be*

Lovingly nurture the plant, either indoors or out in the garden. As the plant grows, so will the love between you and your beloved.

Penstemon Red Riding Hood

Plantaginaceae

Keyword: Courage

These amazing flowers come in a rainbow of colours, and each has their own set of meanings. The other name for these amazing flowers is beardtongue, and they are found all over the world in their varied forms, though they are native to North America. Here we are looking at the bright red variety called red riding hood. Quite appropriate as Red Riding Hood was a rather courageous child when you think about it.

Penstemon Red Riding Hood Courage Spell

If you have a battle ahead in anything—love, relationships, career, finances, or even law—and cannot find your courage, invoke the strength of this amazing flower. Try to find a picture if you cannot grow it. On the day before your battle, hold out your palms, look at the penstemon, and say,

Penstemon, flower of fight
Grant me strength to do what's right
Sending courage with all your might
Let me win this battle outright

Look at the flower, at its bright red colour, and imagine courage flowing through you. Close your eyes and try to see the flower in your mind's eye. See the red and feel that red flowing through you. During your battle, if you feel your courage failing, remember that colour and the flower to ignite your courage again.

Peony
Paeonia
Keyword: Passion

The peony is a beautiful flower that only blooms for a short time. The enormous heads of these flowers come in stunning shades of reds, whites, and pinks. The red peony is a wonderful plant for love, romance, and passion magic.

Peony Passion Massage Oil Spell

Use this massage oil for a night of love and hot romance.

Ingredients

1 ounce or 30 millilitres of apricot oil

9 drops of peony essential oil

A dark glass bottle

Method

Pour the apricot oil into the dark bottle and add the peony essential oil. With each set of three drops, say these words:

> *One, two, three, my love and me*
> *Four, five, six, love and sex*
> *Seven, eight, nine, passion is mine*

Shake the glass bottle a couple of times and then enjoy.

Poppy

Papaveraceae

Keywords: Physical energy

The magnificent poppy is a fantastic plant with phenomenal abilities to help humans with physical pain. Many have written of the tears of the poppy or the milk of the poppy, which are slightly different. The milk can be made from poppy seeds that are soaked in hot water and then crushed to emit a white liquid, hence milk. The process is one of repetition, but an easier way is to go to a Lithuanian food shop, as poppy milk is a traditional drink or soup. Poppy tears are from the opium poppy seedpod, which exudes a white sap called latex when cut.

Poppy Power Spell

If your energy has been low due to pain, worry, or stress and you are feeling physically exhausted, cast this spell. Draw a bright red poppy with a black centre, and as you draw the flower, recite this spell over it:

> *I wax and wane*
> *I feel nothing but pain*
> *Power flow through me*
> *Fill me with red fire energy*

After, pour yourself a small glass of milk, or your substitute milk (I use soya). Imagine the power of the flower flowing into you as you drink the milk. Colour in your poppy and concentrate on your colouring until you feel physically energised.

Red Rose

Rosaceae

Keywords: Love, romance

There is something eternal about the red rose as it speaks to lovers everywhere, and yet the rose can also mean sacrifice or the martyr in not only love, but in life. There is no other flower more renown for love than the rose. Florists the world over even run out of roses on Valentine's Day.

Rose Decision Love Spell

This is a spell for when you want love to come into your heart but have no idea what you are looking for, or what exactly you need. Make a cup of rose tea (buy from your local health food store or pour boiling water over a few rose

petals and steep for five minutes). Light a red candle and sit quietly. While slowly sipping the tea, say these words:

Goddess Aphrodite, help me please
Fill my heart with love
Show me the one who is meant to be
Help me find the one I need
Let them come now, let them come to me
An' it harm none, so mote it be

See what happens in the next couple of days; perhaps you will meet someone, or you will realise what it is you are looking for. If you are still undecided after three days, repeat the spell with the candle and tea for seven nights.

Rose Passion Come to Me Candle Spell

Buy a red candle and anoint it with rose, lavender, and jojoba oil. If you can make the candle yourself, put three drops each of these oils into the red candle and wait for it to set. Now place a needle halfway down the candle. As you push the needle in, envision the person of your dreams coming to you. Light the candle and say these words:

Love, love, come to me
Love, love, set my passion free
An' it harm none, so mote it be

The spell will take effect when the flame reaches the needle, and the person you want will feel the pull toward you.

Sweet Pea

Lathyrus odoratus

Keywords: Romance, marriage

These enchanting flowers with their heavenly scents are native to the Aegean Islands and Cyprus, the island of the goddess Aphrodite. Aphrodite is the ultimate goddess of love, and what a beautiful flower to have from her homeland, the immortal Cyprus. The sweet pea flowers grow in many colours, most notably whites, pinks, blues, and lilacs. It is a climbing plant that twines its way around everything and is best grown on a trellis.

Sweet Pea Marriage Romance Spell

If you are getting married, plant some pink sweet pea and trail them around like a vine. As you plant the sweet pea, say this spell over it, and say it again when the sweet pea begins to grow and you twine them around a trellis:

> *Sweet pea on the vine*
> *Let simple pleasures be mine*
> *Bring my love and me*
> *Entwined together for all time*

The plants will take months to grow, just like a marriage takes years, but growing the sweet pea is all about patience, which is what you need in a marriage. Yet all the effort and patience will be worth it when the sweet pea begins to flower, with its sweet smell of romance entwined within the trellis representing you and your partner.

Other Red Flowers

Here are some additional red flowers you can use in your spells. These flowers can be substituted for those listed in the spells as their harmonics work well together.

Amaryllis

Hippeastrum

The amaryllis is a great plant for love and sex, especially the variety called cherry nymph.

Begonia

Begoniaceae

These wonderfully strong flowers are often compared to roses due to their petals; as such, they can be a substitute in flower spells that require roses.

Clematis

Ranunculaceae

An amazing flower to use in will and determination spells, especially the bright red clematis rouge cardinal variety.

Dahlia

Asteraceae

These are wonderful flowers and come in an array of colours. The bright red dahlia impression festivo is wonderful in all red flower correspondences.

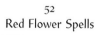

Hollyhock

Alcea rosea

Red hollyhocks are great in spells of passion and sex, especially if male libido is dwindling.

Ice Plant

Delosperma

These beautiful plants are continually in bloom with daisy-shaped flowers and are perfect for all manner of love spells.

Peruvian Lily

Alstroemeria

This bright red lily is perfect in physical energy spells where you need to be in top form.

Salvia

Salvia coccinea

This plant is a wonderful scarlet red and is ideal in all flower power spells.

Tickseed
Coreopsis

This is a perfect flower to use in desire spells, especially the coreopsis Mercury rising variety.

Tulips
Tulipa

Red tulips represent rebirth and are used in spells celebrating everlasting love, such as during an anniversary.

Mystical Beings: Nymphs

The nymphs are a personification of nature as they are spirit manifested in nature itself. Nymphs are tree spirits who protect the forests, the woods, and the eternal springs of life. They cherish nature and celebrate death as a renewal of life. Nymphs stem from Greek mythology and are regarded as semidivine. You could call them the daughters of Gaia, for theirs is Earth to protect and care for. They are indeed the natural florists of the world.

Nymphs are female spirits and are often depicted as beautiful young women who live in natural habitats, usually keeping to the forests and woods. There are many nymphs throughout the world who govern mountains, rivers, and sacred springs, and there are specific wood and plant nymphs who may have different names, such as the meliae, the dryads, or the naiads, to name a few.

Flower Favourite: A Bright Red Dahlia

Asteraceae

The big, bold, beautiful dahlia is the ideal plant for connection with nymphs. Their sensual texture is the embodiment of everything this mystical being represents. Dahlias come in many colours, but it is the bright scarlet variety we are concerned with here. Dahlias represent grace, strength, and an openness to change, and with the added meaning of the colour red, this becomes a formidable flower for use with nymph magic and spells.

Nymph Love Oil Spell

To enjoy and tune in to this wonderful energy is to express your sensuality, be confident with your own sexuality, and channel the energy of the nymph. If you would like to create

your own massage oil that encapsulates the sensuality of the nymphs, try the following.

Add three drops each of rose, juniper, and rosemary essential oil with a base oil of either grape-seed or almond in a dark glass bottle and shake together. Traditionally in each massage oil, you will need at least thirty millilitres of the base oil for a full body massage.

As you shake the bottle of massage oil, say this spell and imagine the night or day you want to have with your partner:

Miss Nymph, bold and free
Uniting love and me
Let us be joined as two become one
Let us have a night of love and fun
Lady Nymph, bless me with sensuality
Help me express my sexuality

Use the oil as needed, including when you are on your own to embrace your own sexuality. The oil will last a year if it is not used. Remember to date the bottle when it is made.

Red is used not only for love, but for many things, and there are so many aspects to love itself. In magic that uses red flowers, physical action is always the result. It is such a powerful colour, and we can tune in to it in so many ways— not only by having a bunch of red flowers in the house, but also by wearing a red jumper or a pair of red shoes. We all need a bit of red in our lives from time to time, so enjoy this vibrant colour and embrace the power by buying a red houseplant, such as a poinsettia in winter or a miniature red rose for the summer.

Orange Flower Spells

Orange flowers are a real powerhouse when it comes to energising and creativity. When used in spells, they can promote confidence and well-being. They also are the flowers of joie de vivre and self-awareness and are excellent when used in a sexuality spell if someone is confused about their sexuality. They are also the best coloured flowers to use for career and are particularly good when used for job promotion or enhancement.

Orange Correspondence Chart

Day: Sunday

Gods: Apollo, Sol, Branwen

Physical: sexual organs, gallbladder, lower intestines, bowels

Crystals: orange jade, fire agate, amber, sunstone, orange calcite

Governs: career, fun, confidence, success, joy, enthusiasm, sexuality, freedom, creativity

The Flowers

Here is a selection of orange flower spells to use along with the correspondences. Remember, if these flowers are not available where you live, use other orange flowers or a photo in place of the actual flower.

Antirrhinum Snapdragon

Antirrhinum majus

Keyword: Confidence

A bright orange-red flower of such beauty and fire that is perfect to use in spells about confidence, especially if you don't speak out at work. If you can, ask the plant for permission to take a flower and cut one flower head away. A photo of the flower will also do.

Snapdragon Know My Worth Spell

Take the snapdragon flower or photo and write out what it is you would like to say in your job on a separate paper. Is it about a pay rise, promotion, or change of hours? Write anything at all. Wrap the flower or photo up in the paper and say these words:

> *I am worth more, here in this place*
> *I can survive this rat race*
> *No more downtrodden I will be*
> *My confidence ignites with positivity*

Keep the paper and flower wrapped up and out of the way until the spell has played out and you have accomplished what you wanted. Then dispose of the flower and spell either by burying it in the garden and giving thanks or burning it safely in a heatproof dish.

Avens

Geum

Keyword: Enthusiasm

Avens are an unusual little plant, but they can be found everywhere from Europe to America to New Zealand. There are over fifty species of this perennial plant, and they can come in an array of colours—white, red, and yellow—but it is the orange varieties that are commonly known. Their colour can range from every type of orange, but the variety totally tangerine or beech house is particularly good for enthusiasm spells, especially if enthusiasm has been waning regarding work, love, or any area of your life that needs a boost.

Avens Activate Enthusiasm Spell

Hold a picture of avens in full bloom and think about the area of life where your enthusiasm is waning. Say,

> *This spell I activate*
> *Let my enthusiasm be great*

Repeat the spell five times as you look at the picture of the avens and notice how they are in full bloom—just completely full of flowers, every space taken up in a cascade of orange. Imagine that this is your enthusiasm; these flowers are your feelings. Then say five times,

I see the flowers in full bloom
Lift my spirits with a zoom

Imagine those flowers flowing through you and imagine bursting into an array of bright orange flowers. When you feel your enthusiasm rising, the spell is complete, but keep the picture handy. Anytime you feel your enthusiasm waning, look at the image once again and meditate until you feel enthused.

Berberis Darwinii

Berberidaceae
Keyword: Enthusiasm

The berberis is commonly known as barberry, and although it's native to South America, it can now be found all over

the world. It is a thorny evergreen shrub that has a cascade of orange flowers, which produce small deep purple berries in the summer. These berries are edible, but they are highly acidic and not very nice. This plant, which was discovered by Charles Darwin during his voyage on *The Beagle* in 1831, is excellent when used in enthusiasm spells.

Berberis Darwinii Exuberant Enthusiasm Spell

If there is a project you need to complete and you are not enthusiastic about it at all, cast this exuberant spell. If you are growing barberry and it is in bloom, gather enough flowers to make a circle around an orange candle. Failing that, have a picture of the orange flowers and sprinkle some Himalayan rock salt around the orange candle in a circle. Raise the candle to the universe and say,

> *Universe, hear my plea*
> *Send abundance of enthusiasm to me*

Place the candle back into the circle of barberry flowers or salt and light it. Look at the flowers and let the candle burn for at least an hour. As it burns, finish your project in view of the candle. If your project requires more time, extinguish the candle after an hour and perform the spell every day until your project is complete. Always work on your project safely near the lit candle.

Bird of Paradise
Strelitzia
Keyword: Freedom

This magnificent flower is quite unique and is a sight to behold. The bird of paradise plant is native to South Africa, but many have it in their homes around the world. It looks exactly like the bird of paradise it is named after, with its orange plumage and blue feathers. Its other name is crane flower because of its resemblance to these birds as well. It is symbolic of freedom and is used in many spells when you want to break free from something, especially an oppressive situation or relationship.

Bird of Paradise Freedom Spell
If you are growing a bird of paradise flower, have it near you in full view as you cast this spell. If not, a clear picture

of it will suffice. Raise an orange candle to the sky in the presence of your bird of paradise and say,

I fly, I fly free, here, there, and everywhere
I fly, I fly free, wherever I may care
Sent by the Goddess for I am a bird of paradise
And my spirit will never ever die

Place the candle near the flower or picture and light it. Look into the flickering flame and think about the situation you find oppressive. Imagine running away from it and feel free, then blow out the candle and watch the rising smoke take your intentions to the universe. A sign will come to you in the coming weeks to help you in your desire for freedom from the situation.

Butterfly Weed
Asclepias tuberosa
Keyword: Self-esteem

This amazing plant is native to North and South America but can also be found around the world. It can attract butterflies and other pollinators to your garden, so it is worth planting. The plant produces clusters of orange flowers from early summer to early autumn. In some ancient cultures, the seedpods were used to create candlewicks, though this is no longer advised, as the plant is extremely toxic and can cause corneal injuries. This plant is perfect for self-esteem spells, especially when someone has made you question yourself.

Butterfly Weed Toxic Person Spell

Sometimes our self-esteem takes a battering from negative toxic people, and although we hear the nursery rhyme "sticks and stones may break my bones, but names will never hurt me," well, they do! It is even worse when it comes from someone whom we think of as a friend, but who needs friends like this? Send this toxic individual packing with a butterfly weed spell.

Write the name of the person who is being cruel on a piece of yellow paper. Have a butterfly weed flower or a picture of one and fold it up in the yellow paper. As you do, say this spell:

> *Your toxic traits I do not need*
> *I ask of you, Butterfly Weed*

Fly them far from me with speed
And restore my self-esteem

Bury the paper and flower in the garden. As the paper disintegrates, the toxic person will have less and less hold over you, and your self-esteem will return.

California Poppy

Eschscholzia californica

Keyword: Success

This must be one of my favourite poppies. Its bright orange petals dancing in the Californian sun bring back fond memories. Due to the wonders of cultivation, this lovely poppy can now be found around the world, though it is native, of course, to California, and is that state's flower. The seeds can be used in cooking and the leaves can be used to garnish food. It is its powerful energy in success spells that I use it for now; it is particularly good for all spells concerning career and creativity.

California Poppy Spell for Success

Sow some California poppy seeds in a little pot and keep it on your window shelf in full view of the sun. Do not cover the seeds with soil as they need light to germinate. Every day for fourteen days, spritz them with some water, and as you do, say this spell over them:

> *California poppies bring success*
> *In all my endeavours, they are the best*
> *Number one I shall be*
> *Glory and money now come to me*

Whatever project you are working on, think about how successful it is going to be. As the poppies begin to grow, so will your success in your chosen field. As they bloom, the spell is complete, but when they start to develop seedpods, keep and renew your spell as needed, or replant the poppies out in the garden, if your weather permits it.

Canna

Zingiberales

Keyword: Joy

Although these plants are natives of the tropics, they can be found all over the world. They look very similar to a gladiolus and are used in agriculture for their high starch properties. Even though they come in wonderful bright colours of oranges and yellows, their seed is used to make a purple dye. However, despite their many uses in manufacturing and agriculture, orange canna are perfect for spells that bring happiness and joy.

Canna Zing Joy Spell

If you are lucky enough to grow orange canna in the garden, collect a couple or take a picture. Arrange them in a vase or look at the picture of them and say,

Canna joy you bring
Making life go with a zing
All my endeavours go bang zoom
Joyful success goes beyond the moon

Concentrate on the endeavour that makes you happy and joyful. Imagine it exploding with an array of orange flowers, which bring success. Keep the flowers for as long as possible; after, bury them in the garden, giving thanks. Do the same with the paper.

Cosmos

Asteraceae

Keyword: Joy

A member of the sunflower family, these wonderful flowers come in an array of colours, but it is the wild vivacious orange colours we are concerned with here. These adorable flowers can be found all over the world, though they are native to North America. They are bound to bring joy to any garden, and it is in this area of mood magic that their power really comes to the fore.

The Whole Cosmos of Joy Spell

Pick a bunch of orange cosmos and pop them in a vase. Place the vase in the room your family uses most: the

kitchen, the lounge, and so on. As you do, say this spell over the flowers:

> *Orange flower of Cosmos Power*
> *Bring joy for many hours*

Regularly change the water of these joyful flowers. The minute they begin to fade and die, say thank you for their joyful energy, and bury them in the garden.

Crown Imperial
Fritillaria imperialis
Keyword: Creativity

This majestic plant is native to the Middle East, though it now can be found from Austria to America. It bears the name *imperialis* as it looks like it is wearing a crown of orange flowers. Although highly exotic looking, it is actually a member of the lily family. It is powerful when used in creativity spells, especially when you really want to show off your creative enterprise and add the "wow" factor to your project.

Crowning Creativity Glory Spell

Light a gold candle and wrap orange flowers around a toy crown, ideally an imperial one. As the flower droops like huge flower gems, it will look great in the middle of the crown. Carefully place the gold candle in the centre of the crown and say,

> *Crowning glory to my eyes*
> *Knowing I will win every prize*

When you are creating something—a painting, book, poem, and so on—wear your crown and enter as many competitions as possible. Leave the candle burning while you enter the competitions and then extinguish it safely.

Foxtail Lilies or Desert Candles

Eremurus
Keyword: Sexuality

These wonderful flowers are simply amazing as they do look like a bushy fox's tail. Their other name is desert candles, and that name is also appropriate. The flowers stand tall on

a slender green stem and can be yellow, white, pastel pink, and, of course, orange. These flowers have been known to grow at least ten feet tall. They are native to Eastern Europe but are also found in Asia, and through cultivation, they are now being found in gardens all over the world. One of my favourites is the variety known as Cleopatra, which has tall orange spikes of flowers. This plant is perfect for use in sexuality magic, particularly when someone is unsure of their sexuality.

Desert Candles Light Sexual Path Spell

This spell requires an orange candle, a mirror, and a picture of the orange foxtail lily. Light the candle and stand the picture near the mirror. As you look into the mirror, say these words:

Eremurus, show me what others do not see
Show me the path of my sexuality

Stare into the mirror, and intermittingly glance at the picture of the tall orange flower. By the light of the flickering candle, an image or sign will form within the mirror.

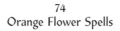

After the spell is complete, say thank you and extinguish the candle safely.

Ginger
Zingiber officinale
Keyword: Career

The ginger plant and its flower are truly spectacular to behold. Although a native to Southeast Asia, it has since spread the world over. The health benefits of this plant outweigh its difficulty to grow in cooler regions of the world. The root of this plant is what many people associate with its healing factor. However, most if not all of this plant finds its way into both culinary dishes and herbal remedies in communities around the world.

Ginger's healing benefits for colds, flu, and stomach upsets are legendary, as is its ability to cure fevers and sore throats when combined with the fresh taste of lemon. Its magical properties are endless, and it is especially beneficial when used in career spells.

Ginger Career Boost Spell

If your career is down in the dumps and no longer fills you with enthusiasm, try to reignite that flame by making a ginger boost drink. You can either buy ginger tea at the supermarket or chop half a fresh ginger root and boil it in two cups of water; after twenty minutes, strain it into a cup, and add some honey to sweeten. As you wait for the ginger to boil, look up the picture of the ginger flower. As you slowly sip your ginger drink, keep the image of the ginger flower in your mind, and then write down why your job no longer inspires you and what needs to change. After, say this spell:

This is what I want, ginger please bring
Make my career go with a zing

Look at what you have written and give yourself seven weeks to see if things change. If they do not and you are still feeling down, think about a different career choice and start applying to jobs that make you feel excited.

Lantana

Verbenaceae

Keyword: Fun

These aromatic flowers are native to the tropical regions of Africa and the Americas. Through cultivation, they now can be found everywhere. The wonderful thing about these flowers is that they change colour as they mature, so the yellow and orange varieties change to red and deeper red the older they get. It is a lovely plant that embraces festival frivolity and fun.

Lantana Lammas Fun Festival Spell

As this plant can flower from spring to autumn, it can be used for an array of festivals. The festivals during this time are Beltane, Midsummer, Lammas, and Mabon; Lammas is the ideal festival for this plant. Plan a Lammas BBQ and invite all your friends. If possible, grow the orange lantana in a plant pot and place it in your patio or wherever you are having your party. Before everyone arrives, touch the plant and say,

My party will be in full spring
Full of joys the festival brings
Lantana plant, begin the fun
Enjoy the party, everyone

After the party, thank the plant and tenderly care for it by giving it water and feed.

Lily

Lilium

Keyword: Confidence

Lilies are found all over the world in all their many forms but are originally a northern hemisphere plant. There are many marvellous forms of lily, from the Madonna to the tiger lily, and all are equally wonderful in all areas of magic and healing. The fierce orange of the tiger lily is perfect for confidence spells. Confidence is something that grows with experience, especially where it concerns work. However, we need confidence in all areas of life, from relationships to work, to dealing with friends and lovers—basically, everything has to do with confidence. If you feel as though you are lacking in confidence, try this spell, though it is a spell that will take your time and patience.

Tiger Lily Confidence Spell

Buy a couple of tiger lily bulbs and plant them in a deep pot. Write out in an orange pen or on orange paper the word *confidence* and bury the paper in the plant pot. Make sure it's not covering the lily bulbs. Recite this spell over the pot:

> *I live in the shade, dear tiger lily*
> *Confidence I ask you bring to me*
> *No more being shy and silly*
> *I will show my confident personality*

Look after your potted tiger lilies and don't forget to water them. As they grow, so will your confidence; when they bloom, so will you.

Nasturtium

Tropaeolum

Keyword: Career

This bright flower comes in oranges, reds, and yellows—all colours that are synonymous with career, creativity, and confidence spells. Though nasturtium is just as versatile in its uses as it is in its magical properties. This plant is found around the world and is a probable native of South America as it is found high up in the Andes, especially in Chile. It is a hardy little plant that can survive extreme temperatures and altitudes. Nasturtium has many culinary uses and is often found in salads and compared to watercress. Its seed-pods can be placed in a spiced vinegar and used like capers. Incidentally, one of its names is poor man's capers, which is unfortunate.

In herbal medicine, nasturtium is an antibiotic and is often used in respiratory and urinary tract infections. Further, it is good for getting rid of unwanted pests and guests in your garden, so many gardeners plant it as a natural insect repellent to protect other plants from nuisance crawlers.

Nasturtium Career Spell

In magic, nasturtium can be used in a career enhancement spell like this one. Have a packet of nasturtium seeds and a pot. Plant the seeds and recite this spell as you do:

> *Help me Gaia in my career*
> *Enhance my role and power*
> *Increase my productivity*
> *Bring job promotion to me*

Tend to the seeds and watch them grow. When they have flowered, your career spell is complete.

Orange Blossom
Citrus sinensis
Keyword: Success

Orange blossom is the sweet-smelling flower of the orange tree. It is so highly fragrant when mixed with water that it is used in many perfumes and culinary dishes. The orange tree is sensitive to frosts and cold weather and so prefers

more temperate regions of the world, such as the Middle East, Florida, and California to name but a few places that grow oranges on a commercial scale. Though many homes in the northern hemisphere now grow miniature citrus plants, including the orange, which can have many blossoms on it throughout the year. The saying with citrus trees is, "The smaller the fruit, the more it blooms." So, you could end up with a never-ending supply of orange blossoms, which are perfect for success spells.

Orange Blossom Boost Success Spell

If there is something you need to be successful but you are unsure of how to bring in a profit, call upon the orange blossom to boost your success. Place five gold or silver coins and an orange blossom (real or photo) in a little orange bag, tie the bag, and recite this spell over it:

Show me success
In my business
Orange blossom boost
Make it go with a boom
My profits will go zoom

Hang the orange bag in a place where you work on your business; it could be a home office or a place of work, including your car if you use it for business, but tie it somewhere out of sight. Leave it for at least a month (though I know people who leave it up for a year) and renew the spell each financial year with a fresh orange blossom.

Red-Hot Poker

Kniphofia

Keyword: Self-esteem

A lovely plant that's stunning to look at, with its varying shades of orange in a large spike of bright flowers. These plants with their amazing flowers produce large amounts of nectar, which attracts bees and birds to the garden, including the equally amazing hummingbird. This powerful plant is perfect for boosting self-esteem, especially self-worth, and realising how wonderful and unique you are.

Red-Hot Poker Unique Spell

Look at the image of the red-hot poker or, better yet, a real one, if you are growing them in the garden, and write seven

positive things about yourself. Think about all the things you can do, such as read, write, work, care for people—but do not compare yourself to others, and do not think you haven't accomplished anything, because you have. After, look at your seven positive things and say,

I am precious and unique
I am full of beauty and mystique
Plenty want to know me for I am true
And I am wonderful to view

Look once more at the red-hot poker flower, how it stands so tall amongst the other flowers. It is no wallflower, and neither are you. Now look at your list and let your uniqueness and self-esteem wash all over you. Feel strong and proud in your unique place in the world. Then fold up the image and list and place them in a safe place where others will not see them. If at any time you feel your self-esteem waning, take out the list and perform the spell again.

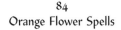

Trumpet Vine

Campsis

Keyword: Sexuality

Trumpet vine is native to North America and Asia—in particular, China. It is a beautiful flower that really does look like a trumpet and comes in loud, bright orange colours. It is really a perfect flower for announcing something and brings an added strength to sexuality spells, especially if friends or family cannot accept your sexuality.

Take Me as I Am Loud and Clear Spell

If there is someone who does not accept you, perform this spell. If you are growing trumpet vine, ask the plant for permission to take a flower; if not, an image will do. Write down the name of the person who cannot accept you. If it is a whole family, just write the surname. Holding the flower like a trumpet to your mouth, say these words:

> *Take me as I am*
> *Love or leave me*

I am what I am
So, love me or let me be

Wait three weeks to see if their attitude toward you changes; if not, perform the spell again. You can do this spell up to three times, but after that time, if they still haven't changed their behaviour and attitude toward you, I'm afraid it's time to walk away. You have given them the opportunity to change, but now you must concentrate on you. Wish them love and happiness but say goodbye.

Other Orange Flowers

Here are some additional orange flowers you can use in your spells. These flowers can be substituted for those listed in the spells as their harmonics work well together.

Aloe Vera
Aloe barbadensis
We always think of the benefit of the green leaves from this plant, but it can in fact have flowers—big, beautiful orange ones. The aloe vera is a perfect plant for success.

Bulbine

Bulbine frutescens

A powerful little perennial plant that is great in confidence and sexuality spells.

Cacti

Lobivia jajoiana

A prickly green cactus that blossoms massive, gorgeous flowers. Ideal for success and career spells.

Coppertops

Crocosmia

An orange plant that has tall slender flowers on a thin green stem. Ideal for self-esteem and confidence spells.

Gerbera

Gerbera

A beautiful bright orange flower that is perfect for freedom spells, especially the variety revolution orange.

Helenium

Helenium

A beautiful flower that is bold and looks straight at you. It is perfect for fun and joy spells.

Lion's Tail

Leonotis leonurus

A wonderful flower for any garden and one that can be substituted for all the correspondences orange flowers govern. Ideally suited for success, sexuality, and freedom spells.

Strawflower

Xerochrysum bracteatum

An amazing flower of remarkable beauty that is ideal for all career and creativity spells.

Succulent

Kalanchoe

A beautiful exotic succulent that blooms bunches of orange flowers. A perfect plant for self-esteem spells.

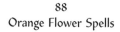

Trumpet Honeysuckle

Lonicera sempervirens

A powerful flower for sexuality and freedom spells.

Mystical Beings: Dragons

Dragons have been written about in every culture and society in the world. The earliest descriptions and writings of dragons are seen as far back as the fourth millennium BC. Many people believe that the dragon myth stemmed from the discoveries of dinosaur remains by early humans. The physical description of the dragon is almost identical to that of a lizard or a long snake with wings. Dragons are generally larger than elephants and are regarded as having long fangs and twin horns. It is generally agreed that most dragons are covered in scales, though there are some who have leathery skin. Their colours can also differ—anything from red to green, black, or orange being the most common.

Flower Favourite: Bright Orange Snapdragon
Antirrhinum

The bright orange snapdragon breathes fire at its very core. This beautiful flower with its long stem of buds almost gives the impression it will spurt fire at any moment. It is no surprise that this flower represents power and is used for many spells to build strength in leadership. Here, we are going to use it to enhance our creative power as the colour orange represents creativity and imagination.

Dragon Creative Power Spell

Dragons embody every correspondence of orange flowers, creativity in particular. If you are embarking on a creative project, invest in a little dragon statue and place it where you work. Before you begin your artistic project, hold the dragon statue in your hands and say,

> *Every time I sit here to work*
> *Ignite the creative spark*

Bring lots of creativity of dragon power to me
Let my work shine with glory

Place your dragon statue back on your desk. Every time you sit down to work, rub its wings and head to ignite the creative spark.

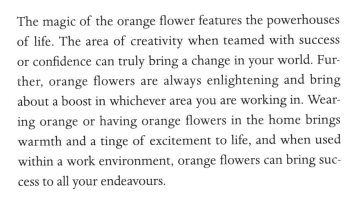

The magic of the orange flower features the powerhouses of life. The area of creativity when teamed with success or confidence can truly bring a change in your world. Further, orange flowers are always enlightening and bring about a boost in whichever area you are working in. Wearing orange or having orange flowers in the home brings warmth and a tinge of excitement to life, and when used within a work environment, orange flowers can bring success to all your endeavours.

Yellow
Flower Spells

Yellow is a colour that is found all over in nature, and yet so many shrink from using it, either in the clothes they wear or in decorating. My mother always had a yellow kitchen, and therein lies the clue of correspondence. The kitchen was always the meeting place in our house, and so what better colour to paint it than yellow, which is known for its happy, chatty, and optimistic vibe. In flower magic, this colour signifies the ending of harsh winters with the bursting of yellow daffodils, crocuses, and aconites carpeting the earth. It is a colour that repels negativity, just as the flowers

93

repel the cold winters with their yellow warmth of the sun. Yellow also repels envy and spite.

Yellow Correspondence Chart

Day: Wednesday

Gods: Mercury, Hestia, Tyr

Physical: digestion, liver, nausea, gallbladder, skin problems, nervous system

Crystals: yellow zircon, golden labradorite, yellow jade, lemon quartz, gold, yellow calcite

Governs: memory, logic, communication, examinations, study, concentration, entrepreneurship, vacations, repelling envy and spite, revealing deception

The Flowers

Here is a selection of yellow flower spells to use along with the correspondences. Remember, if these flowers are not available where you live, use other yellow flowers or a photo in place of the actual flower.

Angel's Trumpet

Brugmansia

Keywords: Secrets, revealing deception

This highly intoxicating plant is found in tropical zones. It is native to South America, particularly Venezuela and Chile. It has now become naturalized in Africa, Australia, Asia, and North America, particularly Florida and Hawaii, with it becoming a sacred flower for the latter.

Angel's trumpet is highly toxic; it is part of the deadly nightshade family. Every part of this plant is poisonous, especially the seeds and leaves, which can lead to death when ingested. However, some cultures, such as the Northern Peruvian shamans, use this plant for initiation and divination rituals. It is a uniquely beautiful and unusual-looking plant that emits a strong sensual fragrance in the evening. It comes in an array of colours, from white to red to pink to a bright canary yellow. It grows best in frost-free zones, though it appeared in many Victorian conservatories and orangeries with other specialized plants. In summer, they can be left outdoors, and in Northern climates, they are better grown in a container.

One legend regarding this magical plant is its connection to the dead. It is said that if this plant becomes fragrant during the daytime, someone close to you has died. If you continue to smell the scent, you may see their ghost.

Revealing Deception Angel's Trumpet Spell

By the light of a yellow candle, sit in front of a mirror. Holding a photo of the yellow angel's trumpet flower, say into the mirror,

> *Shed light upon those who would do me harm*
> *Unveil the shadow from within and ignite the alarm*

Sit quietly and attentively look into the mirror, watching the flickering images as they appear. A name, a face, or even an initial may appear. Blow out the candle and keep looking into the mirror as you see the rising smoke, which can also form into an initial or sign of deceit that only you will understand. After, keep the photo and spell handy in case you need to repeat the spell in a few weeks or months.

Bird's-Foot Trefoil

Lotus corniculatus

Keywords: Anti-spite, anti-jealousy

This common flowering plant is found in many gardens around the world and is a member of the pea family. It has many names, from eggs and bacon to bird's foot and deer-vetch. It is a perennial plant like clovers. It has five leaves, but the middle three are held above the others, hence the name trefoil. Though it looks pretty, this plant is highly poisonous and produces cyanide. Because of its magical number properties, five and three, it is perfect for spells, especially ones involving defence.

Bird's-Foot Trefoil Repel Envy Spell

If someone has been spiteful to or full of envy toward you, cast a repel spell on a Wednesday. If possible, have a bird's-foot trefoil flower or plant. A picture will suffice, but the real thing is best. You also need a mirror, a yellow pen or yellow paper, and ideally a piece of yellow or gold cord, but white will suffice.

In the light of a yellow candle, place the bird's-foot trefoil next to the candle and write the culprit's name on a piece of paper. Stand the mirror behind the flame so you can see your own face as well as the bird's-foot trefoil and tie a knot in the middle of the cord. Take the flower or picture and the paper with the person's name and wrap them together by binding the knotted cord around them. Look at your reflection as you do and say this spell:

I bind you, [name], here and now
No more your envy and spite
Repelling your negativity, I vow
Sending back to you with all my might

Keep the candle burning for as long as possible before extinguishing it properly. Keep the flower, name, and cord all wrapped up for as long as that person is cruel to you. If they remain a problem after seven weeks, perform the spell again, after which dispose of everything by either burying it in the garden or safely burning it in a heatproof dish.

Crocus

Crocus sativus

Keyword: Concentration

This highly prized spice was used as far back as the seventh century BC in the Assyrian region. It has been traded for over four millennia. This little flower is probably the most expensive plant ever to be recorded due to its colourful stigma and styles, which are often called threads.

Saffron crocus has many uses, including culinary, but it is also used as a dye and herbal remedy and is highly revered in magical religious traditions.

Crocus Cookie Concentration Spell

If there is something you must concentrate on, but you seem to be going off target all the time and finding something else to do, make some concentration cookies with saffron. You can make the cookies from scratch or use premade cookie dough. Before you bake, add three pinches of saffron to the mixture, then cook as normal. As you fold in the saffron and stir, say this spell:

With these cookies I do make
Concentration within I will bake
Focus on one intent
Let all my time be well spent

When the cookies are baked, leave them to cool, and then eat one at a time when you have to concentrate on something. Only eat a maximum of two at a time, as you could become obsessive with your concentration and forget everything else.

Daffodils

Narcissus

Keywords: Enterprise, entrepreneurship

Vibrant yellow daffodils brighten any room. Therefore, it is no surprise that these glorious spring flowers mean joy and happiness. They also indicate new beginnings and eternal life and are perfect for entrepreneurs and starting up a new business. All that power and energy that accompany the spring can be used for your new business enterprise.

Daffodil Entrepreneurship Spell

Bring success into your business by having daffodils in your house either in a vase or growing in a plant pot. Say this spell over them and make sure they are the first thing you see when you wake up in the morning. If you are working from home, make sure to have a vase of them in the home office or the place where you work.

> *Daffodil bright, flower of Spring*
> *Leave the success you bring*
> *Make my business go with a zing*

For the first seven weeks of your business, make sure you keep fresh daffodils around your home and the office, and when they start to fade and die, immediately throw them out. Do not have any wilting flowers anywhere near your new business.

Honeysuckle
Lonicera

Keywords: Holidays, vacations

Honeysuckle is a native to the Northern Hemisphere. It is a beautiful sweet-smelling plant that opens its creamy yellow flowers in the evening for pollinating moths. It can be grown anywhere in the garden, from containers to walls and fences. This plant is a climber and needs to explore.

Honeysuckle was often regarded as protecting the garden from evil. Further, because of its sweet scent, it was often thought it could induce dreams of love and passion. But one of the most enduring beliefs regarding this delightful plant is that if this plant is brought into the house while in bloom, a wedding will soon take place in that household.

Honeysuckle Travel Spell

Although, it represents happiness, the honeysuckle is often used in travel and vacation magic. So, before you go on holiday or travel the world, cast this spell to make sure you remember those closest to you.

The night before you are due to begin your holiday, go into the garden with your camera and, standing beside the honeysuckle, say these words:

> *Wherever I may wander*
> *Wherever I may roam*
> *Let me always remember*
> *Those close to home*

Take a picture of your house and keep it in your camera until you return.

Marigold
Calendula officinalis
Keyword: Memory

Marigolds grace many gardens around the world, yet these beautiful flowers are not just to be admired; they can also be used in culinary dishes and healing potions and balms. They are also like a clock, for these bright flowers open at nine o'clock in the morning and close again at around three o'clock in the afternoon. They thrive in full sun and prefer

light, sandy soil. They can be found everywhere in the world on both waste and cultivated land, on arable land, and by the sides of roads. Marigolds are perfect for memory spells, especially if you have forgotten where you have put something or you know you have to do something important but cannot remember what or when exactly.

Marigold Memory Sugar Spell

Create some marigold memory sugar and always have it on standby to help you remember that which you have forgotten. In an airtight container, place a small bag of sugar with seven marigold petals. Pop the lid on and give the container a shake as you say this spell:

> *My memory I have lost*
> *There's something I have forgot*
> *Restore my memory in this hour*
> *Nature's sent, marigold power*

Label and date your marigold sugar and use as needed. The next time you have forgotten something and it is niggling inside your brain, stop frantically running around the house and instead make a cup of tea or coffee. Put one teaspoon of the marigold sugar in the drink and stir widdershins (counterclockwise). Slowly drink the tea or coffee and allow your memory to restore, returning what it is you have forgotten.

Rudbeckia Pincushion

Dracopis

Keywords: Exams

The name *Dracopis* stems from the Greek *drakon*, meaning dragon. Thus, any word with the beginning *draco-* is a term connected to the dragon. The rudbeckia is a beautiful daisy-like flower with a pincushion centre. A good flower to dry, and it goes well in a display with blue cornflowers. Good for spells to do with the family and children, especially only children, or *les enfant unique*, as the French say. And rudbeckia is especially good with all exam spells, whether the exam is for driving, academia, or work.

Rudbeckia Examination Spell

Write down what your exam is for (e.g., driving test, maths test, work). Hold one rudbeckia in your left hand and the piece of paper in your right hand and say,

> *Dracopis, I call upon thee*
> *Bring exam success to me*
> *I ask with all your might*
> *Grant me answers right*

Fold the flower up in the paper and keep it with your books, or notebook, or whatever you have been studying from. Only get rid of this spell when you have taken the test and after you have received your results; do not throw it out before. Give thanks to the flower and bury it in the garden or sprinkle salt over it before disposing of it.

St. John's Wort
Hypericum perforatum
Keyword: Study

This versatile plant has many uses and legends attached to it. However, though it is native to Europe, it is often regarded as a nuisance and seen as an invasive weed due to its behaviour of taking root and taking over gardens. St. John's wort got its name for its flowers being harvested around the time of the summer solstice, which occurred during St. John's Feast Day on June 24. As such, this little plant with its bright yellow flowers would be hung around the house to ward off evil spirits, ill health, and general bad luck.

Its uses as a medicinal herb to help mood swings and regulate PMS and menopausal conditions found popularity in the 1980s. It was still prescribed by herbalists in the 1990s for depression. It has been used by those who work in magic for its positive effects in emotional and stressful situations. So, carry a flower in your purse or pocket to brighten you up when you are having emotional difficulties. It is incredibly useful when you have to study and can enhance your thoughts with positive mental clarity.

St. John's Wort Study Spell

Make a cup of St. John's wort tea, which can be bought from a health food shop. Light three yellow candles and have them

placed in a triangle on your desk or table or wherever you study. Place both palms upon your books and say,

St. John's Wort, Flower of Mind
Help my thoughts to hold in time
Forever encased with knowledge abound
Study good, all safe and sound

As you study, slowly sip the tea and keep the candles lit as they will help you focus. After, if the candles are still burning, extinguish them safely.

Sunflower

Helianthus annuus

Keyword: Communication

The flower of the sun that turns its head to follow the light throughout the day is truly a magnificent flower. Sunflowers are well known to get rid of toxins in the soil, and infused sunflower water, when used as a spray, absorbs negative residue left by toxic people in your home. Sunflowers can also enhance positivity in a legal matter. If there are two or more warring partners in a fight and harmony needs to prevail before they can move forward, such as during a divorce, cast a sunflower positivity spell to help them be at least amicable and positive toward one another. The sunflower's ability to enhance positive communication is second to none, and it is this powerful energy we are going to connect with through the sunflower spell.

Sunflower Communication Bag Spell

You will need a small yellow bag. You could make it yourself, but it must be a natural material—nothing synthetic. In it, place seven sunflower seeds, a small lock of your hair, yellow ribbon, and three drops of sunflower oil. After you have placed everything in the bag, tie it up and say,

> *I have trouble speaking my mind*
> *Let me be positive and kind*
> *I never communicate clearly*
> *Help me speak freely*

Hang the bag in the corner of the place where you do the most speaking, such as in the kitchen, your office, or

even your car. Whenever you feel you are not speaking clearly, reactivate the bag by repeating the spell.

Viburnum
Viburnum lantana
Keyword: Logic

This is a wonderous shrub or tree, and each flower head is made up of a mass of tiny flowers. It has many different varieties, and some have differently coloured berries in autumn. In magic, we use viburnum for defence spells and protection. We make a paste from the berries, which we spread along the doorstep. Viburnum is also used to treat asthma and is an antispasmodic, but be incredibly careful and always be certain of what variety you are growing, as this plant can be highly toxic. It is also good for clarity and logic spells in which you try to make sense of things.

Viburnum Logic Spell
If there is a project you need to work on or you need to think logically on a task but your mind flits all about, go

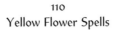

for a walk in nature. If there is a blooming viburnum tree growing, circle it three times and knock on the trunk and say,

> *I need to think straight*
> *Logical reasoning now activate*
> *Pure, concise, and full of clarity*
> *Logical reasoning, now come to me*

Continue your walk. When you get back home, start on your project and think clearly. If you are working on a desk, knock three times to activate your logical reasoning. Every time you feel your mind wandering, knock three times on a hard surface.

Other Yellow Flowers

Here are some additional yellow flowers you can use in your spells. These flowers can be substituted for those listed as their harmonics work well together.

Dandelion
Taraxacum officinale
There are many varieties of this plant, and it is believed to have evolved about thirty million years ago in Eurasia. The dandelion, literally lion's tooth in French, is rich in vitamins A and C, iron, calcium, and detoxifiers, which explains its common inclusion in medicines. Dandelions are particularly good at repelling spite and envy and equally good in spells concerning revealing deception.

Goldenrod
Solidago
Goldenrod is a wonderful plant that umbrellas over one hundred species and can be found in meadows and prairies across the world. They are exceptionally good in all communication spells.

Hibiscus
Malvaceae
This amazing flower, which is used in many countries as a drink, is also found in paper products and herbal medicine.

It is perfect for communication spells and all magic involving concentration and memory.

Ranunculus
Ranunculaceae
This wonderful versatile flower comes in over six hundred species and is otherwise known as buttercups. It is ideal for all types of spells within the correspondences of yellow flowers.

Tansy
Asteraceae
Tansy is a member of the aster family and is found all over Europe and Asia. It is ideal in logic and reason spells.

Water Lily
Nymphaeaceae
The water lily is a beautiful aquatic flower found all around the world. It is particularly good for all manner of communication spells, including difficult ones that concern partnerships.

Yarrow
Eriophyllum confertiflorum
This plant is native to California but is found all over the world in its various forms. It is good in study and examination spells when retaining information is difficult.

Yellow Hellebores
Helleboreae
Hellebores, otherwise known as Christmas roses, are a good addition to memory spells.

Yellow Hyacinths
Asparagaceae
Yellow hyacinths are spring flowers and are usually called yellow queen. They have the beautiful smell of hyacinths, and this variety is particularly good when used in entrepreneur and business spells. Hyacinths also represent jealousy, so they are ideal for envy spells.

Yellow Orchids

Orchidaceae

Orchids are beautiful plants that are very delicate and can be quite tricky to grow, especially in the northern hemisphere, but many people keep them as houseplants. They are good in vacation and entrepreneur spells.

Mystical Beings: The Muses

In Greek mythology, the nine daughters of Zeus are called Muses. The Muses inspire mortals in great works of art, with individual responsibilities for all aspects of the arts, from drama to music, painting, writing, and even astronomy.

They are the inspiration for the word *museum*, which means house of the Muse—house of inspiration, creativity, and magic. And museums around the world truly are all these expressions of human thought, as is entrepreneurship.

Flower Favourite: Mimosa

Mimosa

A beautiful yellow flower with a sweet wonderous smell. A favourite with the enchanted beings of the fairy realm and a favourite of the Muses, who inspire creativity. Mimosa is good in communication and creativity spells, especially those concerning inspiration for a business.

Mimosa Muse Inspiration Spell

If you would like to start up your own business and become an entrepreneur but have no idea what you would like to do, ask a Muse for inspiration.

Get a pen and a notebook, place a lit yellow candle next to the notebook, and have a small vase of mimosa next to you. If you cannot get any fresh mimosa flowers, their coloured image will do.

Looking at the mimosa, say these words:

Mimosa Muse divine, breathing beauty of nature's breath
Breathing inspiration into me, imagination set free

Stare into the flame and write what you see, feel, smell, and hear. Then set about making your business a reality by researching it as a side hustle or even as your main career. Keep your options open and do not be surprised if you get a couple of ideas coming your way. After, extinguish the candle safely and keep the fresh flowers in the house for as long as possible. Once they start to fade, offer your gratitude to them, and bury them in the garden.

Yellow flower spells have a whole range of correspondences, and many focus on mental clarity. They can be used in so many spells, especially academic ones; therefore, placing a little bunch of yellow flowers in your dorm or where you study is ideal. I always thought libraries or offices should have yellow flowers to enhance learning and communication. Further, when yellow flowers are brought into the house, they bring happiness and optimism. Use yellow flowers for the correspondences listed and embrace this wonderful vibrant colour.

Green
Flower Spells

Green flower spells are full of luck, positivity, and wealth. Green is the colour of physicality and all things pertaining to that, including beauty and strength. In this area of magic, trees and the grass itself are used in many spells in addition to green flowers. Further, in this colour, we find many herbs used in spells as they are predominately green.

Green Correspondence Chart

Day: Friday

Gods: Venus, Freya, Diana

Physical: heart, lungs, respiratory system, viruses, blood pressure, infections

Crystals: malachite, vesuvianite, moldavite, green aventurine, amazonite, green jasper

Governs: wealth, horticulture, environment, luck, commitment, beauty, competitions, money, physical strength

The Flowers

Here is a selection of green flower spells to use along with the correspondences. Remember, if these flowers are not available where you live, use other green flowers or a photo in place of the actual flower.

Christmas Rose

Helleborus argutifolius

Keyword: Wealth

Hellebores are brilliant flowers that bloom throughout the winter from late autumn to early spring. As its name implies, it will be in full bloom during the Christmas or Yuletide period. Hellebores come in many varieties with different colours, but this one is best for flower magic and has green bowl-shaped flowers. Christmas rose is ideal for any type of wealth or abundance spell.

Hellebore Three Wishes of Wealth Spell

If there are three areas of your life where you want abundance and wealth, cast this spell on a Friday night. Use three fresh flowers or photos of them. On green paper or using a green pen, write down three areas of your life where you wish for abundance; for example, wealth in relationships, wealth in spiritual areas, or wealth in business acumen. You can ask for financial wealth, but why waste a wish when you can do a separate money spell? After you have written your three wishes, say this spell. As you do, hold the three bowl-shaped flowers or their photo in your hand and say this spell over your wishes:

Hellebore flowers, I ask of you
Grant three wishes of wealth
From me to you

Carefully roll up the paper with the flowers or photo inside and keep the roll in a safe place until your wishes have come true.

Chrysanthemum

Asteraceae
Keywords: Physical strength

Chrysanthemums are one of the commonest flowers and are a favourite with florists the world over. These wonderfully versatile flowers come in an array of colours, but it is the green variety, such as green mist or Anastasia green, that we are concerned with. Furthermore, just as there are many varieties and colours, there are also many different names. I know them as the pom-pom bush. In flower magic, they represent the Goddess and strength and are very good for boosting physical strength if you have been

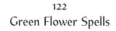

unwell. Place a vase of fresh green chrysanthemums in the room and feel the energy they bring.

Green Chrysanthemum Goddess Strength Spell

Pick a small chrysanthemum flower with care and place it on a window ledge to capture the moon and the sun. Leave for three days. On the third day, say over the flower,

> *Sun and moon caught in your power*
> *Chrysanthemum threefold bring your strength to me*
> *An' it harm none so mote it be*

Put the flower in your purse or sports bag. Every time you need physical strength, touch the flower and count to three.

Cymbidium Orchid
Cymbidium goeringii
Keywords: Money, finance

There are many different types of orchids, but in this green section, we are concerned with the boat orchid. We need

the green flowering variety, which was originally found in East Asia. The orchid is a beautiful flower but has hardly any uses apart from some species that are used in cooking. However, in flower magic, the orchid is particularly good in money and wealth spells.

Cymbidium Money Spell

Pluck three petals from the plant or take photos of the flowers and place them in your palm. Clasp your hands together. Say this spell:

> *Clean and fresh money shall be*
> *Flowing from the universe to me*
> *I need money in times of three*
> *Hurting none, blessed be*

Place the petals in your purse, and within times of three—which could be anything from three hours to three days, weeks, or even months—money will come to you from an unrelated source.

Flower Jasper

Keyword: Horticulture

Horticulture is not just about the plants growing in your garden, but about what is growing inside, too. Houseplants often are overlooked in horticulture spells, but I would like to take this opportunity under the green flower correspondences to tell you about an important horticulture elixir you can make.

This magical stone has a base colour of cream with varying shades of pink, red, white, yellow, and green; for horticulture, try to get most of the green variety. Green flower jasper is often compared to a flower bouquet and given at handfasting ceremonies to the bride.[2]

The flower jasper has considerable power, not just for gardens, but for many physical conditions, too, such as kidney and glandular disorders. It is also a power stone for those

2. Handfasting is a wedding ceremony, an example of which can be found in *A Spellbook for the Seasons* (Wellbeck Publishing, 2019).

who are feeling sad and depressed as this stone is a mood enhancer and a general happiness stone. Flower jasper may also help mend a broken heart. Further, it can uplift a serious workplace by its presence.

Crystal Flower Elixir Horticulture Spell

Create flower jasper crystal elixir water and spray it onto your houseplants for added energy to keep them healthy.

Fill a jug with cold water and place the flower jasper in the water. Leave it for at least an hour or overnight. In the morning, carefully remove the stone and pour the water into a spray bottle. Spray your houseplants with this magically infused water. Say this spell while spraying the elixir over your plants and garden:

> *Gentle flowers meek and mild*
> *From tame to the wild*
> *Indoors, outdoors, and everywhere*
> *I will look after you with care*

Jack-in-the-Pulpit

Arisaema triphyllum

Keyword: Competitions

This amazing green flower is native to North America. It has three flowers that grow together at the top of one long stem and curl over to give the effect of a tube-looking flower. It is strange and unusual but is a powerful plant to use when going in for competitions.

Jack-in-the-Pulpit Competitions Spell

If there is a competition you are eager to win, print out a picture of the green jack-in-the-pulpit and sprinkle some fennel seeds on it as you say,

> *Competitions galore*
> *Let me win a whole lot more*

Roll up the photo with the seeds inside and place the roll over the competition entry for one night before posting the competition. If it is a lottery ticket, roll both the

photo and the ticket up together and leave until the lottery is drawn. After, keep the photo of the jack-in-the-pulpit, but the fennel seeds need to be thrown on the garden. Remember to thank them.

Lady's Mantle
Alchemilla alpina
Keyword: Beauty

Alpine lady's mantle is one of those rather extraordinary species of plant that is a hermaphrodite: the seeds develop without being fertilised. Alpine lady's mantle is native, as the name suggests, to the Alps, but can be found across many parts of Northern Europe. It has several uses within herbal medicine, especially for gynaecological disorders. I use it as an ingredient in glamouring spells. Glamouring is a form of magic that involves spells to change one's appearance to appear more aesthetically beautiful.

Lady's Mantle Glamourous Beauty Spell
If there is a special occasion, call upon the ancient goddesses of love and beauty for help. Have a picture of your favour-

ite celebrity you want to look like and sprinkle some green lady's mantle flowers over it, reciting this spell as you do.

> *By the power, Astarte, Ishtar, Hathor, and Aphrodite*
> *Let the beauty of all flow to me*
> *Shining bright for only this night*
> *An' it harm none, so mote it be*

Roll up the picture with the petals over it and enjoy your night. Afterward, dispose of the photo and flowers either by using water or burying them in the earth.

Primroses
Primula
Keyword: Luck

Primroses are found the world over in many different guises and many different colours; they have been cultivated and have many hybrids. For this area of flower magic, we need the variety that has green flowers, such as the beautiful green

lace, which was developed in Ontario.[3] Green lace has a beautiful flower with a lime-yellow eye and darker green frilly petals. When planted in borders, this plant gives a delicate sensual quality to the garden. Within flower magic, primrose is ideal for luck spells and enhancing anything with positivity and good vibes.

Primula Luck Spell

If there is something you have been wanting for some time in any area of your life, create a luck spell using a green primula. In a tiny green material bag, place three primula flowers and say,

> *Little luck bag, please grant me*
> *Luck wherever I may be*

Tie up the bag with a green ribbon and hang it in a room where you spend most of your time. Keep it up for

---

3. Primula green lace was bred by Sandra Tuffin in Ontario. https://www.rainyside.com/plant_gallery/perennials/PrimulaGreenLace.html.

no more than a year, after which perform the spell again if you need some more luck.

Wallflowers

Erysimum

Keyword: Commitment

Wallflowers have over one hundred fifty species and are part of the cabbage family. Wallflowers come in many colours, from pale blues to pinks, reds, oranges, and greens, to name but a few. This plant's blooms span the rainbow. However, for our purpose here, we require the green flower variety, which is *Erysimum capitatum*, which can have a lime-green flower.

Wallflower Commitment Spell

The power of wallflowers to continue to grow in a whole range of places and climates embodies the commitment of this strong plant. It is an ideal plant to use in spells that require longevity in commitment; for example, it can help with tasks that are proving difficult in your career or legal

battles. Wallflowers can also be good in spells requiring commitment in a fitness regime or diet.

Write down what you need to commit to on a piece of paper. For example, *I will stay on my diet.* Then, holding the green wallflower in your hand (real or photo), say this spell:

> *I am committed to this task*
> *I will work on it to the last*
> *Let nothing stop me until I finish*
> *My commitment will not diminish*

Repeat this spell every morning for two weeks until you start to see the benefit of your commitment. Anytime you feel like giving up, take out the flower photo or cut yourself a bunch of wallflowers and reaffirm your commitment by repeating the spell.

Zinnia
Zinnia elegans
Keyword: Environment

The zinnia flower is a member of the sunflower family and comes in a variety of colours, including the beautiful giant green Benary's giant lime species. It is a big bold flower that is used in environmental spells and grows to about twenty-five inches (sixty-four centimetres) tall.

Zinnia Earth Environment Help Spell

In the evening, just before it gets dark at twilight, plant three giant lime zinnias in your garden or in a plant pot. Raise your hands to the sky and breathe three deep breaths. After, kneel to the ground and place both palms upon the earth. Say,

> *Hear me, Earth*
> *Your child am I*
> *Planet of my birth*
> *I dwell under your sky*
> *I give to you as you give to me*
> *I embrace your strength and beauty*

In return I will protect and serve thee
Ask of me what you wish
An' it harm none, so mote it be

When you go to bed that night, be aware of the dreams you have, as you may receive messages from the earth or images that ask you for help.

Other Green Flowers

Here are some additional green flowers you can use in your spells. These flowers can be substituted for those listed in the spells as their harmonics work well together.

Angelica

Angelica

This beautiful flowering plant is edible—its other name is wild celery. You can use its roots and stalks in aromatic teas and green salads. It is also ideal in physical strength and competition spells.

Cockscomb
Celosia

This amazing plant looks like it should be in the ocean as its shape is reminiscent of coral. It is perfect if you are creating a mermaid garden.

Envy Zinnia

Zinnia elegans

A perfect plant for all manner of repelling spells; it is also good with spells concerning age and especially youth. It is a great drought-resistant flower that blossoms annually. It has a large flower that blooms in a lime tone and over time turns a beautiful green.

Flowering Tobacco

Nicotiana alata

A beautiful plant with leafy, full-bodied green stalks that create a foundation for the small green flowers at the top. A beautiful addition to the garden, but not ideal for animals or children as it is poisonous.

Green Anastasia Spider

Dendranthema grandiflorum

These plants come from the daisy family. Ideal for environment and nature spells. The flower petals are long and thin and resemble spider legs, hence the name.

Green Dianthus

Dianthus barbatus

A wonderful plant that is perfect for commitment and luck spells. Quite a rare plant. It has green fuzzy ball-shaped flowers that have a spicy fragrance.

Lady's Slipper Orchid

Orchid cypripedium

This flower, which is predominately found in Canada and the Eastern United States, is a truly beautiful and unusual flower. Great in beauty spells and excellent in all spells involving wealth and money.

Mediterranean Spurge

Euphorbia characias

This delightful evergreen perennial shrub has an array of greens and is truly a sight to behold. Its bottom leaves are a dark green whilst the large flower has clusters at the top that are a bright neon green.

Viridiflora

Rosa chinensis

This plant is the oldest known variety of rose in the world. Unlike other roses, it has no scent. It is ideal in beauty and luck spells.

Mystical Beings: Leprechauns

Leprechauns are part of spirit within the domain of the earth and are often described as small people. Their physical characteristics have been changed throughout the centuries, and today we view leprechauns as males dressed in green and sitting on toadstools. Yet this image is a modern-day

mixture of pixie, elf, and fairy, while the original leprechaun was nothing of the kind.

In the eighth century, leprechauns made their first appearance in the tales of Ireland. This was the time when people first began to write oral legends down, yet the leprechauns, as with so many physical manifestations of spirit, have been with us for much longer. There were leprechaun women, too, and they do not sit on toadstools either, for that matter.

What we do know about leprechauns is that they are native to Ireland and live in the hills and mountains in a secret, sacred, enchanted world only they can find using their shillelaghs. The shillelagh is a short, thick club that was carried as a defence against muggers and thieves. It is also known as a cudgel and is still popular with people today for the same purpose. Many depictions of leprechauns show them with their shillelaghs, and given that this was a weapon, one can deduce that a leprechaun would defend himself at any cost. Their trade is shoemaking, and they are fiercely protective of their pots of gold.

Flower Favourite: Bells of Ireland

Moluccella laevis

A simply stunning plant with tall stems and a mass of bell-shaped flowers. A perfect plant for those whose garden respects the Celts. Bells are the musical instruments of fairies, so this is a wonderful addition to a fairy garden. A good flower with spells and potions intended to make greater contact with the enchanted world, particularly with beings of Ireland, such as the leprechauns.

Leprechaun Invocation Spell

If you wish to connect with the energy of the leprechaun, plant bells of Ireland, clover, heather, ferns, or shamrock in the garden, ideally in an old pair of Wellington boots. A word of warning with shamrock: it is a notoriously difficult plant to grow outside of Ireland, but it's extremely lucky if you manage to grow it. On a Friday night, cast this spell. Plant your plants in your old Wellies or pot and say over them,

Enchanted beings of the earth
Elves, gnomes, and leprechauns, too
Let us not forget those Irish makers of the shoe
Handing out love and luck
Not letting nature run amok
I invoke you now in this moment, in this time
Bring good fortune with this rhyme
Welcome to you here in this space
Teach me all you know here in this place

Lovingly tend to the plants every day and notice the strange little things appearing and happening in your garden, such as flowers appearing that you have not planted, or garden ornaments moving around.

—◆●●●●◆—

The magic of green flowers is a powerful force within their designated correspondences. Their many different hues of green, from the dark leaves of hellebores to the lime-coloured primula, bring a fresh awareness of possibility to everything.

Green flowers are very much physical and are the body of many plants. Explore and experiment with green flowers in all areas that pertain to the physicality of life, from money to luck to nature and the earth herself.

Blue
Flower Spells

Blue flower magic is the embodiment of so many important parts of life, from business and leadership to healing—and not just healing of the body, but also of the earth. One of the correspondences we find under this area of magic is peace in all its forms, including world peace and peace in the home. Blue is the colour that features in many peace organisations' flags and symbols as it embodies tranquillity and serenity.

The blue flowers we use in this area are predominately the lighter blue we find in nature as the deeper blue, indigo, is connected to legal and educational correspondences. When using blue flowers for health, try to find ones that are light blue-turquoise.

Blue Correspondence Chart

Day: Thursday

Gods: Odin, Mercury, Hermes, Isis

Physical: thyroid gland, throat, fevers, teeth, bruises, communication disorders

Crystals: turquoise, blue howlite, angelite, blue calcite, aqua aura quartz, blue quartz

Governs: health, leadership, prosperity, business, expansion, peace, trust, promotion, mending family quarrels, teenagers

The Flowers

Here is a selection of blue flower spells to use along with the correspondences. Remember, if these flowers are not available where you live, use other blue flowers or a photo in place of the actual flower.

Bluebonnets

Lupine

Keyword: Promotion

Lupine originates from the Latin word *lupus*, which means wolf. Many of our ancient ancestors used to eat bluebonnet seeds, and today they are found in many culinary dishes throughout the world. Bluebonnets, or lupins as they are also called, are perfect for promotion spells, especially when you are going to be promoted to a management or leadership position.

Lupin Promotion Spell

Gather the seeds of a blue lupin and write in blue pen on a piece of paper what your leadership role will involve—for example, line management, governing people, delegating tasks and roles, and so on. Sprinkle the seeds over the paper as you say,

> *Lupin standing bright and tall*
> *Grant this promotion for me above all*

I work hard both day and night
So, my promotion will be right

Think for a while what that leadership role will be like and imagine yourself in it. Then carefully roll up the seeds and keep them in a safe place before you get the leadership role.

Bluestar

Amsonia

Keyword: Peace

Bluestars are native to North America, though they are found throughout the northern hemisphere. They are beautiful little plants that bring harmony and peace as they embody strength and endurance. Any flower that has five petals and comes in the shape of a star is considerably more powerful than any other flower as it resembles the pentagram, our most sacred symbol—a sign of protection, defence, love power, and spirit. For this reason, the bluestar is an ideal flower to use within spells and magic relating to peace and the desire for peace, especially on our little blue planet.

Bluestar Peace Full Moon Spell

If possible, grow bluestars in a little pot; if not, a photo will suffice. Have a picture of Earth and light a blue candle. Hold out your palms, and in the flickering light of the candle, say,

> *Blue planet of my birth*
> *Fragile yet strong*
> *Sad but full of mirth*
> *I pray and ask upon you, bluestar*
> *Bring the beauty and the peace*
> *Let all heartache and wars cease*
> *Blessed bluestar, I ask of you*
> *Bring this all into view*

Meditate upon the flame and imagine a world where peace and love prevail. Imagine the picture of the earth being surrounded by a glowing white light of healing and peace. Let the candle safely burn for a while, but never leave it unattended. If it does not burn itself out, blow it out and watch the rising smoke take your intentions to the universe.

Blue Lotus

Nymphaea caerulea

Keyword: Trust

The blue lotus was revered in ancient Egypt and was thought to belong to the goddess Isis. The Egyptian Great Mother was worshipped throughout the whole of the ancient Roman world, and her worship continues to this day.

This sacred plant is a water lily found on the banks of the Nile. It has been used since ancient times as both a sedative and a perfume. Its main purpose is in aromatherapy. Its religious importance was central to many ancient Egyptian rituals involving the pharaoh and his connection to the gods, especially Isis.

In the Goddess pentagram, Isis is in the east; she is blue and associated with water (for the Nile). Her stone is the beautiful blue lapis lazuli, and her symbol is the tyet, or knot of Isis, like the ankh.

Blue Lotus Goddess Ritual Cleansing

If someone has betrayed your trust, the emotional exhaustion you feel because of the betrayal is painful. If you are exhausted and spiritually and emotionally drained, create a ritual of cleansing and purification. Make a ritual bath with five drops of essential rose oil and five drops of lotus oil (any lotus oil, as blue is notoriously difficult to find). Light two blue candles and soak and meditate in the bath. If you do not have a bath, put five drops of essential rose oil and five drops of lotus oil into your shower gel and shake it up. After your ritual bath or shower, over the blue candles, say these words:

> *Mother Isis, I call upon you*
> *I have been betrayed and need to renew*
> *Blessed waters of the Nile*
> *Wash me clean and cleanse my soul*
> *Let me rest for a while*
> *Help me restore*
> *The trust I had before*
> *Cleansed of pain, pure forevermore*
> *Mother Isis, blessed be*
> *An' it harm none, so mote it be*

Isis is the Great Mother and a great goddess of magic. Be respectful and always give thanks by placing a rose or lotus on your altar when good little things happen to you.

Cornflower

Centaurea cyanus
Keyword: Leadership

Beautiful blue flowers that look good everywhere and can be dried and used for a long time. To dry cornflowers, cut a bunch of twenty or so and tie it together. Hang it upside down in a warm dark place until the stems are stiff enough to support their beautiful heads. This usually takes a week or two. Store them until needed, but make sure you wrap them carefully, and do not let stems tangle.

Cornflowers are excellent for not only health spells but also for ones that involve leadership and managing a team or project. They are helpful when dealing with a boss or leader who is being cruel or dismissive and who doesn't believe in you and your abilities.

Cornflower Leadership Spell

If you have a boss who doesn't show any interest or positivity toward your work, cast this spell on a Thursday. Write the name of your boss on a piece of paper in blue ink, light a blue candle, and have a blue cornflower nearby (a photo is fine). Hold the flower or photo in your left hand and the name in the right and say,

> *Cornflower blue, Cornflower blue*
> *Believe in me as I believe in you*
> *Your lack of interest in all I do*
> *Is a reflection of you*
> *I cast this spell to open eyes*
> *To see the merit in all I do*
> *My work will win the prize*

Roll up the name and, by the light of the candle, burn the paper. I do burn spells over the sink as it is the safest way to get rid of the ashes, but you can use a heatproof dish or your cauldron. Extinguish the candle safely.

Gladiolus

Gladiolus

Keyword: Business

Beautiful gladiolus flowers in late May or early June. They are full of amazing colours, including a beautiful blue. These flowers are a favourite amongst fairies and elementals. Their tall stems sway in the gentlest of breezes, giving them the appearance of dancing. They are great flowers to use in all types of business spells.

Gladiolus Business Wish Spell

If you are lucky to have gladiolus flowers growing in your garden, go out at night and say this spell over them. Then whisper your business wish into the gladioli or use a photo of a beautiful blue gladiolus. Touch the gladiolus and say,

Gladioli dancing bright
Grant me a wish this night
Let my business shoot to the stars
Shouting louder than a pulsar

Look up to the night sky and imagine your business beaming and glowing like the stars. Name the brightest star in the sky after your business and watch it glow. Every time your profits slump or your business hits a snag, perform the spell again.

Glory-of-the-Snow

Chionodoxa luciliae

Keyword: Prosperity

This fragile little plant is made of strong stuff as it is one of the first plants seen after the long harsh winter. It is originally from Turkey but can be found everywhere and planted as bulbs in the autumn, ready for the forthcoming spring. The blue variety is a wonderful plant for all manner of spells that concern prosperity in finances, love, or health.

Glory-of-the-Snow Prosperity Spell

Grow some glory-of-the-snow bulbs in a little pot, ready for spring. Before you put the soil in, write on a small piece of paper, *prosperity*. Put the paper in the pot and then the soil

and plant the bulbs as normal. After, hold the pot in both hands and say,

> *I call forth Prosperity blast*
> *Come to me at last*
> *Venture forth and bring a lot*
> *Trebling all of what I got*

Imagine your energy flowing into the plant pot, igniting the bulbs to take root. After, lovingly care for the plants and watch them grow. As they grow, so should your prosperity, culminating in their flowering.

Himalayan Blue Poppy

Meconopsis betonicifolia
Keyword: Health

These magnificent blue poppies are a very hardy plant originally found in the Himalayas. Poppies are used in many remembrance services, especially the blue poppy, which is used to remember the animals who have passed during war and conflict. This amazing little flower is ideal in many spells regarding health and becoming the best version of yourself.

Blue Poppy Health Spell

Sow blue poppy seeds in a plant pot. Say this spell as you sprinkle the seeds on the soil:

Poppy health I call to me
Bring forth the best version of me
I embrace health and longevity
An' it harm none, so mote it be

For the next six weeks, eat healthy, exercise, and go for a walk every day. If you drink and smoke, stop for the entire six weeks. Embrace and take ownership of your health whilst tenderly caring for your poppy plant. When your poppy plant blooms, your health will have improved.

Hydrangea

Hydrangea macrophylla

Keyword: Expansion

Hydrangea comes from Greek and means water vessel. Nothing could be further from the truth as these plants need lots of water; as soon as they become dry, their leaves start to droop considerably.

Hydrangeas come in a variety of colours, from lime greens to whites to pinks to purples, but I believe the blue variety is the most beautiful. They really are an amazing flower as it is possible to make pink hydrangeas bloom blue flowers by changing the pH of their soil. Many gardeners have said that applying coffee grounds to the soil changes their pink hydrangeas to blue.

Given their propensity for growing large blue flower heads, they are ideal in all spells relating to expansion, whether for business, career, family, health, relationships, or even social media following.

Hydrangea Expansion Spell

This is a generic spell in which you can write your desired area of expansion. If possible, always grow a hydrangea plant as they are quite useful in a range of spells. Create a display of these gigantic flowers; cut only one as that is all that's needed and place it in a strong vase. Write on a piece of paper what you want to expand and, holding the paper in your right hand while looking at the blue hydrangea flower, say,

Big and bold
Bright and free
Let this [area] *grow expansively*

Carefully put the paper underneath the vase and tenderly keep the water level up. When the flower does eventually die, the spell is complete, and your expansion will be complete. Bury both the dead flower and the paper request in the garden, giving thanks.

Love-in-a-Mist

Nigella damascena
Keywords: Quarrels, family

This beautiful little flower is time honoured in any cottage garden. The many seeds contained in its ornamental seedpods are self-seeding like poppies, so be careful. Love-in-a-mist is perfect for all manner of family spells. Simply bring a vase of the cut flowers into the family home and ask them to bring harmony to all who dwell within.

Love-in-a-Mist Family Quarrel Spell

Sprinkle one of the seedpods along the entrance of the house and say,

> *My family is in a twist*
> *I ask of you, Love-in-a-Mist*
> *Let quarrelling be in the past*
> *Bring family harmony that will last*

Leave the seeds at the door for seven days. If the family arguing has stopped, clean and hoover. Every time the family starts bickering and arguing, perform the spell.

Phlox

Phlox

Keyword: Teenagers

A wonderful flower of May favoured by the enchanted world. Phlox comes in a multitude of colours, from blue to pink, red, white, and violet. They are also very fragrant. Phlox are favoured by the Fae as they are a popular food source for all manner of wildlife, from rabbits to groundhogs. They are also popular with butterflies and moths. Phlox are good for friend and relationship spells, especially those concerning teenagers and young adults.

Phlox Teenager Friendship Spell

If friends have not spoken to you for a while and you want them to reconnect, try this reconnection spell using phlox. This spell does not control someone's will; it instead ignites their thoughts of you, which they then can act upon if they wish. Have a vase or plant of phlox nearby or say this spell in the garden. Hold a photo of the friend in your hand as you say,

> *Phlox, phlox, phlox*
> *Let [name] hear my knocks*
> *Let their friendship never end*
> *My thoughts to [name] I send*

If you are sat at the table performing this spell, knock three times. If outside, knock three times on the ground. Wait twenty-four hours before repeating the spell. Do it once more and then pick up the phone and call them if they have not already called you in that time.

Other Blue Flowers

Blue Daisy
Felicia amelloides

This beautiful blue daisy bush is an evergreen plant originally from South Africa. It is often called the blue kingfisher plant, given its lovely blue colour. It is a great plant to use in all spells to do with business and prosperity.

Brunnera
Brunnera macrophylla

Brunnera flowers look like forget-me-nots, but the leaves are greatly different. These flowers are native to Eastern Europe and Asia, and they have large hairy leaves. They are ideal when used in prosperity and promotion spells.

Clematis
Ranunculaceae

It is hard to believe, but the clematis belongs to the buttercup family. It is an amazing plant that comes in the rainbow. The blue variety is amazing when climbing up a wall or fence.

They are often used in spells concerning peace and mending family quarrels.

Desert Bluebells

Phacelia campanularia

These beautiful blue flowers are often called California bluebells and are native to the Mojave and Sonoran Deserts. However, through cultivation, gardeners around the world are enjoying their beauty. The lovely little flowers are perfect for magic that involves trust issues after betrayal.

Flax

Linum lewisii

Flax is a delicate blue flower that originates from North America. The flowers have five petals, which makes it ideal for all manner of blue flower spells, but it is especially good when used in health magic.

Gentian

Gentiana

This beautiful blue-flowered plant is striking to see as the flowers grow in a trumpet shape; once fully opened, they have five petals. They are ideal in all manner of blue flower spells but are especially beneficial for health and bringing peace.

Hyacinth

Hyacinthus

Hyacinths are originally from the Northern Mediterranean area. These heady-scented, beautiful spring flowers are ideal in expansion and leadership spells.

Morning Glory

Convolvulaceae

These pretty little flowers come in a variety of colours, but the sky-blue variety is particularly beautiful and, as the name implies, flowers early in the morning. These plants are ideal in magic concerned with health and peace.

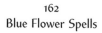

Periwinkle

Vinca minor

The lovely periwinkle is a member of the dogbane family and has another name many are familiar with, which is myrtle or creeping myrtle in the States. Its flower has five petals and is ideal for all manner of blue flower spells.

Sea Holly

Eryngium planum

This amazing little plant that grows near coastal areas is native to Europe and Central Asia. It is a blue thistle that has silvery-blue stems, and it is an extremely magical plant. It is excellent in all magic concerning teenagers and mending family quarrels.

Mystical Beings: Fairies

This little elemental being is central to hedgewitchery, and their presence in nature combined with the good work they do in the garden is something special. Fairy rings are bare patches of soil that appear in the garden after fairies have been dancing in a circle; these are thought to be lucky.

Although, you are advised not to step inside as the fairies might take revenge.

Flower Favourite: Campanula

Campanulaceae

Campanulas are often called bellflowers as *campanula* is Latin for little bell. The Fae adore everything that makes a sound, especially bells. This is one of the ways they can be summoned. These beautiful little flowers come in the brightest blue colour nature can give us. They can be found all over the world now, and some have been cultivated to last for most of the spring and summer. If looked after well, they will bloom from April right through to October. Campanulas are great for not only contacting Fae but also for a range of spells found in the correspondences for blue flowers.

Fae Sight Water

Cut a flower head of campanula and place it in a bowl filled with water. Leave overnight in view of the full moon. In the morning, pour the water into a spray bottle and bury the flower in the garden after giving thanks to it. Spray the water around yourself when you need a boost in contacting the Fae, saying,

Show me what I cannot see
Elementals and the fairy

Anytime you wish to interact with and see the Fae, spritz some of this water around and see what happens.

------●●●●●------

Blue flower magic is as rich in flowers as it is in correspondences. There are so many areas within this beautiful colour that it is difficult to summarise. From the big and bold hydrangea flowers to the delicate blooms of glory-of-the-snow, blue flowers can be found anywhere and everywhere. When planted in a garden, they create their own sacred corner of nature with their peaceful beauty, and when brought into the house, they harmonise the environment with their energy.

Indigo
Flower Spells

The deep blue of an indigo flower is a sight to behold, and many appear almost black when the flowers begin to mature. Indigo is reminiscent of the night sky and features so subtly within the rainbow of life. Yet here is where we find the areas of the mind and mental health. Indigo is such a transitionary colour that it becomes the path or the hedgerow itself between the mind and the soul, where we begin to leave the area of mind and body and enter spirit.

Within this section, we find travel and long-distance travel. We also find new beginnings, education, reconciliation, and

compromise. Let us begin at one of indigo's most fundamental correspondences: law, and all that pertains to it.

The area of legal matters is rather large and can refer to many areas of life if not all. The legal complications of money, career, health, love, and marriage, with the ultimate legal battle being divorce, can be difficult to deal with. Tribunal, court cases, litigation, mediation, and arbitration are just some of the ways legal matters spill into our lives and world. Yet even in the cold hard reality of this subject, the strength of flowers can be used to soften the effects and create a positive outcome.

Indigo Correspondence Chart

Day: Saturday

Gods: Loki, Cerridwen, Hades

Physical: brain, scalds and burns, eyesight, communication disorders, high blood pressure

Crystals: lapis lazuli, covellite, tanzanite, lazulite, blue apatite, cobalt aura

Governs: mental health, legal matters, justice, long-distance travel, home, education, reconciliation, nurturing new beginnings, adaptability, compromise

The Flowers

Here is a selection of indigo flower spells to use along with the correspondences. Remember, if these flowers are not available where you live, use other indigo flowers or a photo in place of the actual flower.

Birdbill Dayflower
Commelina dianthifolia
Keyword: Reconciliation

The birdbill dayflower plant is such a delicate little flower, and yet it is incredibly strong as it can withstand the extremes of weather from droughts to floods. It has been used as an aphrodisiac for cattle and to strengthen the body after the ravages of an illness, though this is no longer recommended as the plant can be toxic to humans. This exquisite flower

found in the Southwestern United States and Northern Mexico is perfect for reconciliation spells when two warring parties need to forgive and forget and move on together.

Birdbill Dayflower Reconciliation Spell

If you have been the victim of a bully at work, or there has been a war between you and a friend or partner, use this spell to reconcile. Lighting one white candle and one indigo candle, sit in front of a mirror with a picture of your enemy and a picture of the birdbill dayflower and imagine them in front of you. Let the candle flicker as you say,

> *Battered and bruised we have been*
> *Underhand and devious, powers unseen*
> *I call upon you, Birdbill Dayflower*
> *I invoke your special power*
> *Two enemies now reconcile*
> *No more the silly fighting of a juvenile*
> *No more the warring factions are we*
> *Peace abound, blessed be*

Stare into the mirror and imagine you and your enemy being friends and doing great things together. After, safely extinguish the candle and enjoy your newfound friend and the peace the situation brings, but keep the photos handy just in case you have to perform the spell again.

Bluebell
Hyacinthoides
Keyword: Legality

The bluebell is a beautiful sight to behold in a spring wood, carpeting the forest during March, April, and early May. Its scent is also exquisite. This favourite flower of Great Britain can be found throughout the world. There are many hybrids of this plant, and the native bluebells of France and the United Kingdom have protection orders on them, making it illegal to pick or uproot wild bluebells. Incidentally, never pick a wildflower, no matter how beautiful it is.

Bluebells are highly regarded both by horticulturists and those who practice magic, and quite rightly so. The bluebell is a gatekeeper to other worlds, and hedgewitches revere

them. They represent truth and are said to bring luck to those who have them growing in their garden.

In a legal battle, the bluebell will keep you in good stead with the powers that be, and the truth will always prevail.

Bluebell Justice Bona Fide Spell

Have a vase of bluebells or a picture of a bluebell on hand and focus your thoughts on it. On indigo paper, write your legal case and woes. Then, focusing on the bluebell, cast this spell. Repeat three times before folding the paper and placing your legal woes under the bluebell plant or picture:

Bluebells, ring out your sound
Ring in my luck
Let truth and justice run amok
Let the bluebell peal
And win my case with zeal

Keep until the case is over and then discard the bluebell by burying it in the garden.

Blue Wild Indigo
Baptisia australis
Keyword: Justice

Blue wild indigo is a beautiful flower native to North America. It is found growing at the borders to woods and forests, along streams, or in meadows. It is therefore a hedgewitch plant, one used for travelling to the border, but it is also incredibly strong in legal magic.

Blue Wild Indigo Affidavit Spell

Blue wild indigo can be used for any legal matter, from finances to business, career, or any wrongdoing in which the authorities have been involved.

For this spell, create your own emblem or coat of arms using the image of the blue wild indigo. Draw a shield shape on a piece of white card. Inside, draw three blue wild indigo flowers. Colour them indigo, or you could use the corresponding chart for the days of the week and colours that pertain to your case.

Holding your crest, say this spell:

Tell the truth and nothing but
Just the facts and nothing else
Justice prevail for myself

Keep your crest in plain sight in your house until the case or tribunal has finished with the desired outcome. Then give thanks to the blue wild indigo crest and sprinkle salt over it, which cleanses it of magic. You can keep your crest if you wish or recycle it.

Columbine

Aquilegia vulgaris
Keywords: New beginnings

Columbine is originally native to Central and Southern Europe, Asia, and North Africa. Today, it can be found in gardens around the world. It can also be found growing in meadows, near forest and beach edges, in parks, and around old house ruins. Since medieval times, every part of the plant has been used in folk medicine. However, columbine is toxic and not suitable for self-medication. It was often depicted in medieval paintings with the Virgin Mary as it was regarded as a religious symbol of purity, and it was considered sacred to the goddess Venus. It also represents the seven gifts of the Holy Spirit: wisdom, understanding, counsel, fortitude, knowledge, piety, and fear of the Lord. It is viewed as a protector against evil and is used in ritual as a guardian of the south.

Columbine Wishes New Beginnings Spell

Plant some columbine in a little pot. Write your new endeavours and what you want the outcome to be on a piece of indigo paper or card and place it under the plant pot.

On a spring morning, go outside and raise your hands to the skies, then reach down and touch the columbine. Say,

> *As above, so below*
> *Columbine be with me wherever I go*
> *Grant me success in my new beginnings*
> *Let my new endeavours always be winning*

After, tenderly care for your columbine. When it flowers, the spell will be complete. However, always continue to

look after the plant as if you forget about it and it dies, so will your new endeavour or beginning.

Forget-Me-Nots

Myosotis
Keyword: Grief

Forget-me-nots are very fragile little flowers that have gained notoriety due to their favourite place amongst certain British royals. These delicate flowers bloom from April to October and are wonderful for any garden. They are good for spells and healing the mind from sadness and depression.

Moving On Spell

If a loved one has passed and you wish to move on, try this spell. Have their picture nearby. Light an indigo candle and hold a little forget-me-not. Say these words:

> *Forget-Me-Not, I ask of you*
> *Though you have gone from my sight*
> *In my heart you shall roam forever in my life*

But now I must heal for my journey continues
Going forward with strength and might

Look at their picture no matter how hard it is and hold the flower. Remember your loved one who has passed. When you are ready, blow out the candle. Watch the rising smoke drift away, place your pain upon it, and watch it go. After, place the little flower with the picture of your loved one and keep them forever in a safe place.

Hyssop

Hyssopus officinalis
Keywords: Mind, health

This beautiful indigo flower is a member of the mint family and was exceedingly popular in medieval physic gardens. It is a great flower to use in mental health spells and potions, especially in an essential oil, which is ideal when applied to a massage oil or a bath.

A Depression Spell

Depression is a serious illness and needs professional intervention, so please always contact your doctor first and discuss the best form of help available. In addition to professional help, try a massage oil made with five drops of hyssop essential oil in fifty millilitres of a carrier oil, such as baby oil, olive oil, or almond oil. Shake it up in a dark glass bottle. While doing so, say,

> *Clouds of sadness swoop over me*
> *I cannot see clearly*
> *Hyssop flowers, release your power*
> *And send me help within this hour*

Massage your legs and arms with the massage oil. If someone can massage you, all the better; do not suffer from depression on your own. This is a time when you need your friends.

Iris

Iris

Keyword: Compromise

This stunning flower is a butterfly magnet, and its Greek name means rainbow, which says it all, really. The iris is also a fleur-de-lis. This symbol has adorned many royal houses throughout Europe for many centuries. No wonder, then, that this flower is connected in magic to nobility and the establishment and notable institutions. Therefore, it is good in financial matters, such as meeting with bank managers, accountants, and tax affairs where a compromise needs to be met.

Iris Compromise Spell

Try this spell if you are having problems in any area that needs a compromise. Have a picture or a painting or a real iris in a vase near you when you cast this spell.

> *Royal Iris, strong and true*
> *Make my matters as noble as you*

> *Both parties will bend and yield*
> *This compromise will secure a deal*

Take a photo of the iris on your phone and have the photo with you when you have your meeting where a compromise needs to be met. Afterward when everything has been sorted, delete the image off your phone.

Lily of the Nile

Agapanthus

Keywords: Travel, protection

A giant-headed flower of an intense indigo that is beautiful in the garden or in a pot on the patio. This flower is ideal for long-distance travel spells. They are native to Africa, but now through cultivation they can be found everywhere from Britain to Australia to California.

Lily of the Nile Travel Protection Spell

If you are going on a long journey, cast a spell of protection around you. On the night before you travel, place a photo of the lily of the Nile flower over your travel documents

(e.g., tickets, passport, etc.). Standing in front of your luggage, say,

> Protect me as I travel far
> By plane, boat, train, and car
> Arriving safely, all is right
> As I travel both day and night

Keep the photo of the flower with you as you travel. Only discard it when you have returned safely home by either shredding it and burying it in the garden or by sprinkling salt over it and then recycling it.

Poor Man's Weatherglass

Anagallis arvensis
Keyword: Adaptability

Another name for this plant is pimpernel, and although many are familiar with the scarlet variety, the deep indigo variety of this plant is spectacular. It is found all over the world in its varied forms. It is truly a remarkable plant and one that changes and adapts to environmental conditions: it

opens when it's sunny and closes when it rains or gets dark. It is no wonder then that the pimpernel is a plant used for adaptability spells, especially when someone finds it difficult to adapt and change.

Pimpernel's Adaptability Spell

Collect three flower heads and place them in a vase. Light an indigo candle on a Saturday evening, and if you are finding it difficult to adapt to anything, reach out and touch the flower heads while saying this spell:

> *Gentle flower, meek and mild*
> *Growing freely in the wild*
> *Send sweet flexibility to me*
> *Help me with adaptability*
> *Help me bend but do not break*
> *Turning round as the pimpernel makes*

Meditate upon the candle for a while and watch how it flutters here and there, left then right at the slightest breeze. Watch the flame change direction without going out and

recognise that is how you need to be. Keep the candle burning safely for as long as possible before extinguishing it.

Vervain

Verbenaceae

Keyword: Education

Vervain is a family of plants that contains over two hundred fifty varieties. It is native to North America and is full of legends and mysteries. It flowers in many colours but has five petals, which personify magic.

Blue vervain has long been associated with supernatural forces, including the dispelling of vampires. In the past, it was called Hera's tears after the Greek goddess. In ancient Egypt, it was called Isis's tears. It was once claimed to be the herb that cleansed Jesus's wounds from the cross, hence it being known as the holy herb. This miraculous herb is wonderful for not only fighting vampires but also for education spells.

Vervain Education Bag Spell

If you're in or returning to school and need a little extra boost, create this spell using vervain and your rucksack or backpack that you carry your books and work in. Bind three bunches of blue vervain with a piece of string, cotton, or ribbon and say,

> *Learning is hard I cannot brag*
> *But I got this education in the bag*
> *Vervain be true and might*
> *I will get all my answers right*

Keep the vervain bundle in your bag. When you get home and do homework, always take the vervain bundle out and leave it on top of your books while you complete the work. In the morning, always be sure to pop the vervain bundle in your bag and keep it for the entire school year. After, if there is anything left, bury the remains in the garden, but generally, by the end of the school year or course, the magic has been spent, and so the vervain bundle will have disappeared.

Wolfsbane

Aconitum

Keyword: Home

This plant has many names, including aconite, monkshood, and devil's helmet. This plant's most common name is wolfsbane and it is often regarded as one of the most poisonous plants of all. It has been given the name of monkshood as it resembled the hoods worn by medieval monks. There are over two hundred varieties of this plant and many of them are highly poisonous and toxic to humans. They range in colour from yellow to white to dark indigo. Wolfsbane is native to the northern hemisphere and must always be handled with caution. Acquiring dry wolfsbane from a reputable herbal or magical store is of the upmost importance.

Home Protection Spell

If you feel you are under attack and need extra protection, create this wolfsbane protective potion.

Mix six pinches of dried wolfsbane with one cup of black salt—either volcanic salt or salt that is ground with charcoal.

Grind all the ingredients in a pestle and mortar, then sprinkle the mixture around the outside of your home, saying,

> *Boundaries and doors, I summon thee*
> *Round and round my property*
> *Keep the evil at bay*
> *Protect therein always*

The power of this spell around your borders will last six months, after which you may repeat the spell.

Other Indigo Flowers

Here are some additional indigo flowers you can use in your spells. These flowers can be substituted for those listed in the spells as their harmonics work well together.

Anemone

Anemonoides blanda

This lovely little blue flower is also called winter wildflower and is an intense blue with a yellow centre. This is an ideal plant to be used in adaptability spells.

Aster

Asteraceae

A beautiful flower with over one hundred seventy species, all with their own unique power. The indigo variety is ideal for all spells involving legal matters.

Blue Star

Aquilegia

An amazing flower with a white star inside a larger five-petalled blue flower. The double flowers of intense blue and white are perfect for both education and justice.

California Lilac

Ceanothus

Although called lilac, the blue variety is indigo. There are over sixty varieties of this plant that can be found all over the world. This plant is perfect for reconciliation spells.

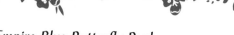

Empire Blue Butterfly Bush

Buddleia davidii

An incredibly intense blue buddleia that is perfect for long-distance spells.

Globe Thistle

Echinops

These stunning flowers have dark blue petals on a spiky frame. The globe thistle is ideal for nurturing new beginnings.

Grape Hyacinth

Muscari

This plant is not to be confused with the heady-scented hyacinth that blooms in the spring. The grape hyacinth is a densely blue plant that produces tiny spikes of urn-shaped flowers. This plant is great when used in compromise spells.

Oxford Blue

Eryngium bourgatii

This amazing plant with its striking blue thistlelike flower is ideal for education and home spells.

Mystical Beings: Pixies

The pixie is a strange one to describe as it is neither fairy nor elf, but a strange mixture of the two. One thing that can be said of the pixies for certain is that they are connected to the Celtic and Pict people of the British Isles. It is said that wherever there is a descendent of the peoples of the British Isles, we are likely to find a pixie.

The pixie's appearance can differ from county to county in the British Isles, but generally they all have pointy ears and translucent wings, which are usually unseen. They do love to skip and run and jump and, of course, fly. Pixies also have a wicked sense of humour and love to play tricks on people, especially lazy people. So, if you are having a duvet or couch potato day and suddenly feel little pinches, it is likely a pixie prodding you to get a move on.

Flower Favourite: Blue Haze Hebe

Hebe

The hebe plant is a native of New Zealand but is now found around the world in its many forms. There are over ninety varieties of this plant, and one of the exquisite types

is the pixie, which is a very deep indigo often called blue haze. The plant itself is very magical and is named after the Greek goddess of youth, Hebe. We plant it for its powerful elemental connections—in this case, to pixies.

The elementals are keepers of great knowledge of not only the earth and nature, but also of life and how they live. So much of our time on Earth is spent worrying about tomorrow, but by communicating with elementals, we can learn to live in the here and now and appreciate the present.

Hebe Pixie Bell Enchantment

As you tend the garden, say this spell. If possible, ring a bell three times. As you ring the bell, say this spell:

Enchanted beings of the earth
Your many guises bring much mirth
Elves, gnomes, and pixies, too
Your splendour brings life anew
Living and working in harmony
Teaching all to love life and be free

The past is past, what is gone is spent
Teach me how to live in the present

Sit for some time in the garden and breathe deeply. Think only about the moment you are in and do not worry about tomorrow. Every time you start to think about the future, come back to nature and spend time in your garden or go for a walk.

—●●●●●—

Indigo is a potent concoction of flower magic that incorporates many correspondences. The area of law and justice in all its many forms is a large part of indigo, as are education and home. Indigo flowers involve the transitional spells of movement and the crossing of the border into the next and final realm of the rainbow, which is violet and pure spirit.

Violet
Flower Spells

Violet is the final colour in our journey through flower magic and the rainbow of nature. Violet within flower magic epitomises the soul and spirit, the Goddess, and the many plants and spells used to ask for her help and guidance. If there was ever a colour that matched hedgewitchery, it would be violet in all its many hues. Here, we find belladonna spells that connect to the Morrigan herself, who is a triple goddess and can appear as the maiden, the mother, or the crone. We begin this section with the deeply

spiritual and supernatural power of belladonna and an explanation of the Goddess herself.

Violet Correspondence Chart

Day: Monday

Gods: Morrigan (a triple goddess), Badb, Macha

Physical: thyroid gland, insomnia, phobias, addictions, allergies to chemicals

Crystals: amesite, tanzanite aura, violan, amethyst, charoite, purple fluorite

Governs: spirituality, imagination, psychic powers, intuition, secrets, animal kingdom, dreams, perfection, hope, charity, transformation

The Flowers

Here is a selection of violet flower spells to use along with the correspondences. Remember, if these flowers are not available where you live, use other violet flowers or a photo in place of the actual flower.

Atropa Belladonna

Belladonna

Keyword: Transformation

Belladonna, or deadly nightshade as it's commonly known, is a plant that features in legends and myths of witchcraft throughout the world. This highly poisonous and misunderstood plant holds such fascination that it can lead the curious to make tragic mistakes. Belladonna is native to Europe, Africa, and Asia and is a relative of tomatoes, potatoes, and aubergines (or eggplant, as it's otherwise known).

Belladonna Transformation Spell

There is another term in magic like shape-shifting called glamour. Originally, a glamour was regarded as a spell cast by a witch to make somebody see things in a different way, but it later came to refer to a spell that literally changes a person's appearance. If you have a battle coming up, a job interview, or any challenging meeting and need to glamour and portray yourself as strong and confident, the best and

the victorious, cast this spell. Place a photo of belladonna under a purple candle and say these words over it:

> *Gracious Morrigan, I call upon you*
> *Change me so that only I can see*
> *The nature hidden within me*
> *Let my appearance be strong and true*
> *I am confident and right to those who view*
> *Great Morrigan, blessed be*
> *An' it harm none, so mote it be*

Balloon Flower
Platycodon grandiflorus
Keywords: Animals, protection

The balloon flower is a member of the campanula family and is native to the Far East, including China and Russia. It has five magnificent petals and is a powerful plant of protection that's also ideal in many health spells. Its roots are used in many herbal remedies, including those for cholesterol

and for people who have weakened immune systems and respiratory illnesses.

Balloon Flower Animal Kingdom Protection Spell

Have a picture of a hot-air balloon and a picture or flower of the balloon flower. Tracing your hand around the picture of the hot-air balloon, imagine soaring in it as it becomes a giant balloon flower. As you do, say these words:

> *High above the world, so high*
> *Balloon flower soaring through the sky*
> *Seeing all on Earth, air, and sea*
> *Protecting all with flora invincibility*

Feel yourself sitting in its little basket as it soars through the sky, as you look down upon all the animals of the world. In the basket are thousands of balloon flowers. You begin to throw them out; watch them drifting to the earth and sea, floating through the air, emitting a power of protection over all the animal kingdom.

English Lavender
Lavandula angustifolia Vera
Keyword: Imagination

Lavender is one of the key ingredients in many herbal remedies, and it is used for a great many spells, potions, and concoctions. It is a perennial plant that can grow up to one metre in height. It flowers in the summer through to the autumn, and the best time to gather the flowers is around July to August. Lavender is so versatile and we use it in many spells, from healing the atmosphere after an argument to creating an imagination spell bag. Any form of lavender can be used, not just English, as the French variety is also very potent in many spells.

Lavender Imagination Spell Bag

You need a little purple bag, some fresh lavender, purple ribbon, and your intentions. On a small piece of paper, write out the purpose of your imagination. Is it for a poem, book, essay? Roll up the little piece of paper with your intentions

and pop all the ingredients in the little bag. Tie the bag with the ribbon. As you do, say,

> *With this bag I invoke*
> *Let my imagination wake*
> *From slumber sleep*
> *Let thoughts dig deep*

Hang the bag up in the room you do your imaginative work in.

Eucalyptus

Eucalypteae
Keyword: Intuition

Many, if not all, eucalyptus plants are native to Australia. Eucalyptus trees have many uses, from making didgeridoos to honey and oils to pulp, which is needed for paper. They are very fast-growing trees, and many use them to clear swamps. They have even been used for prospecting given their intricate root system that draws up gold deposits as well as water. Their leaves and stems have a violet hue to

them, hence their propensity in many violet spells, especially within the area of intuition.

Eucalyptus Intuition Oil Spell

If you need your intuition working, create this massage oil. Mix ten drops of eucalyptus oil with fifty millilitres of a base carrier oil of either jasmine or almond and shake it up. As you shake, say this spell:

> *I think, I feel, I see*
> *Bring intuition to me*
> *Like a light switching on*
> *Conned and tricked by no one*

Massage the oil over your arms and hands and allow it to seep in, igniting your intuition. Keep it in a dark glass bottle and always label and date. Use as needed.

Heather
Calluna vulgaris
Keyword: Dreams

Heathers predominately come out in August and autumn. Heather is mainly associated with Scotland, though Ireland has its fair share of purple, white, and pink heathers. There are many types of heather that can be found in our gardens, parks, and mountains, flowering throughout the year. As a Celt, I adore heather and use it in many spells. It is my go-to flower for many areas of magic.

Heather Dream Spritz Spell

Gather some fresh purple heather and place it in a spray bottle with an amethyst, then pour mineral water in the bottle. Leave it for twenty-four hours before you do this spell as the heather and amethyst need to infuse the mineral water; the longer it is left, the stronger it will become. Spritz your pillow before you sleep. Do not soak the pillow; just a couple of sprays should do. As you spritz, say,

Slumbers deep within the sleep
Of dreams I ask and more
Let me see the life that went before
In future I yearn to see
All that will befall to me
Slumbers deep within my sleep
In dreams I do not weep

When you use the heather dream spritz, always have a notebook next to you. The moment you wake, jot down all you can remember.

Lilac
Syringa
Keyword: Perfection

Once a native of Europe and Asia, lilac can be found all over the world in its various forms and varieties. The divine smell of lilac is a perfect air freshener and is a favourite of the Fae. It is rumoured the Fae make lilac wine for Beltane. Though be warned: lilac wine does not taste how its flowers smell, and, once again, do not use the white flowers as they belong to the Goddess. Lilac is good for so many spells, especially if something you are working on needs to be perfect.

Lilac Perfection Spell

Have your project nearby when you say this spell. If possible, have a bouquet of purple lilac in the house or spritz lavender essential oil around you in a circle. As you do, say this spell:

> *Tipsy-turvy*
> *Turvy-tipsy, upside down*
> *Magic of perfection come to me*
> *Lilac flowers all around*

Take several deep breaths and smell those lilac flowers. As you do, close your eyes and imagine your project finished and written in gold. Begin to work on your project with the flowers nearby and in smelling distance. Do this every time you work on your project until it is finished. Use this spell every time you want something perfect.

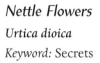

Nettle Flowers
Urtica dioica
Keyword: Secrets

Nettles are found all over the world, and many regard them as a nuisance. However, for others, nettles are incredibly important and are used in a wide variety of ways. In the green flower section, we saw their power for the benefit of a physical commitment spell. Here, we are concerned with their flowers. Nettle flowers are often referred to as Ophelia's flower due to Shakespeare's *Hamlet*. In his time, nettles and their flowers represented life and death, hence their appearance in Ophelia's death garland alongside daisies, crow flowers, and long purples. Crow flowers are another name for buttercups, which signify ingratitude.

Nettle flowers can be either white or a purple colour and can be used to banish negativity and unwanted guests, especially when used in sage sticks. Nettle flowers become increasingly powerful this way in cleansing the home of any unwanted spectral guests. They can also be ground

into a powder and used as hexilium; *exilium* means banish in Latin. We can also call it hexilio. Nettle flowers are also good with secrets and releasing or keeping them, depending on the intention.

Nettle Flower Secret Water

Carefully collect three blooming flower stalks from the nettle plant and wash them under warm water. Leave them to one side on a kitchen towel to dry. After, fill a spray bottle with water and add three teaspoons of salt and the nettle flowers. Tightly place the lid on and turn the bottle upside down three times. As you do, say these words:

> *Secrets here in this place*
> [Open or closed] *now in this space*

Spray your nettle flower secret water wherever and whenever you feel there are secrets that need to be kept or disclosed.

Passionflower

Passiflora

Keyword: Spirituality

Passiflora is a family of plants that consists of over five hundred varieties. The flowers of these plants are extremely beautiful and full of passion, hence the name. Most passionflowers can be found in South America and in Mexico, but they have since been cultivated and can be found throughout the world. There is a distinct blue one that now grows wild in Spain.

The flower itself only lasts a day, so always admire the passionflower when you see it. The fruit that comes after the flower is equally admired for its taste and its versatility in several dishes, from special Asian savoury dishes to the Moorish passionfruit cheesecakes of the West.

In a recent medical study, it was found that certain species of Passiflora performed as well as oxazepam in the treatment of anxiety disorders. This is interesting as those who work in magic have often associated this plant with relaxation and calming the mind.

To connect with your inner voice, it is good to meditate and to be still and quiet. This is hard to do in our busy lives, but you do need to have some "me, myself, and I" time.

Passionflower Spirituality Spell

On an evening when you will be alone, lock the door and turn off phones, computers, and televisions. Make sure you will not be disturbed. Light a purple candle and create a protected sacred space or circle. You can either create a small circle, or you can spray holy water (sea salt and water).

You can create sacred space by placing five crystals you feel close to evenly around you in a circle. In the centre, have a picture or flower of the passionflower. Imagine a wall of protection around you generated by the crystals and the holy water, stemming from the passionflower. When you have created your sacred space and your candle is lit within the circle, sit down and calm yourself, close your eyes, and focus on your breathing. The other way of entering a meditative state is through visualisation of a special place or by focusing your gaze on an object, such as the

flame of the candle or the passionflower itself. When you are content that you are now in a peaceful state, say this spell:

[Universe or Goddess], *help me be wise and true*
Let the right action come through
Help me listen to your voice
I will listen now that I am free
Speak words of instinct and of wisdom
I will embrace my sacred spirituality

Sit or lie down in the circle and listen to your inner voice come through. Think of a problem you have and what you should do about it. You must let yourself be totally relaxed. Listening to your instincts does take a while to learn, so do not be too disappointed if you receive no ideas; you must continue with the meditation ritual and exercise the spirit. Remember, magic is not always easy; some parts are difficult, while others will come naturally.

Violet

Viola odorata

Keyword: Hope

The beautiful blue violet flower means hope and faithfulness and has been used for centuries by lovers. Violet is an evergreen perennial plant and the flower has five scented petals; violet is therefore perfect for magic. This plant grows in fields, hedgerows, woodlands, and gardens around the world. This little plant can grow anywhere, and so can love and, most importantly, hope.

Violet Hope Spell

Buy a violet plant and keep it on your windowsill or somewhere you will see it daily.

> *Hope all around*
> *Hope abounds*
> *For now, and evermore*
> *Hope safe and sound*

Every time you see the flowering violet, know your love is faithful. If, however, the plant begins to wither and die, one of you has been unfaithful!

Viola

Viola sororia
Keyword: Psychic

Viola comes from one of the largest plant families in the world with five hundred species. It is found in northern temperate zones. It is great for secret and psychic power spells. It has been used in herbal medicine and magic for centuries. The flowers and leaves are both edible and were used as a decoction to help with lung complaints.[4]

Viola Psychic Powers Spell

Use this spell to heighten your psychic energies. If you are growing violets in the garden, pick a handful of flowers;

---

4. For a full description of the medicinal benefits of violets and a recipe, see *The Hedgewitch's Little Book of Seasonal Magic* (Llewellyn Publications, 2022).

if not, many health food shops are beginning to sell dried violet flowers. If fresh, wash them, then pour boiling water over them; allow to steep for at least five minutes before drinking. As you gently sip the violet tea, say this spell:

> *Power of the universe arise*
> *Appear before mine eyes*
> *Let me see with eyes anew*
> *As visions come into view*

Slowly drink the tea and allow your mind to open to new experiences and visions.

Wisteria
Fabaceae
Keyword: Charity

Wisteria is an amazing flower that can be found all over the world. Wisteria is a climbing plant and, in many ways, looks like a vine as it twists and turns through climbing frames. Its amazing violet- and lilac-coloured flowers look like bunches of grapes draping down. However, this plant

can be quite invasive; my auntie once grew it, and within five years, it had taken over most of the house outside—but then again, she is a witch! As with many things in nature, wisteria needs to be kept in check, so a good pruning and cleaning is a must with each passing year or season.

Wisteria Charity Spell

One of the practices we do each season is a clear-out, and that includes anything from clothes to ornaments to curtains to basically anything. It is always important to clear things properly, and that includes any psychic residue that may build up over time, especially in the house of a hedge-witch, no matter how careful she is! Therefore, before giving things away, I like to perform a clearance spell.

Go through the things you are going to give away. Using a wisteria flower dipped in water, lightly flick the water on the items as you say,

Sweet charity
I give to you as you give to me

Sweet wisteria on the vine
I release what was once mine

If you don't have a wisteria flower, a couple of sprigs of rosemary or sage will do.

Other Violet Flowers

Here are some additional violet flowers you can use in your spells. These flowers can be substituted for those listed in the spells as their harmonics work well together.

Alpine Betony
Stachys monieri

Alpine betony is a wildflower that is now found all over the northern hemisphere. The tiny flowers have petals that grow up from the middle and resemble feathers. Betony is ideal in perfection and animal kingdom spells.

Bee Orchid
Ophrys apifera
This amazing flower is often regarded as highly evolved due to its deceptive pollination. It is a perfect plant for all areas within violet flower correspondences.

Bush Clock Vine
Thunbergia erecta
This amazing flower is originally from Africa and is now found all over the world. It has a cascade of purple flowers and is ideal for all spells concerned with the animal kingdom.

Cyclamen
Myrsinoideae
A simply stunning flower that is used throughout the northern hemisphere in autumn and winter gardens. This plant is ideal for hope and charity spells.

Diviner's Sage

Salvia divinorum

This amazing plant is connected to both sage and mint. It is perfect for psychic powers and dreams.

Northern Bog Violet

Viola nephrophylla

A simply stunning flower native to North America. A great flower for all spirituality spells.

Pasqueflower

Pulsatilla vulgaris

This beautiful flower is found across the Northern United States and looks like crocus. It blooms in the spring. The pasqueflower is ideal for imagination spells.

Petunia

Solanaceae

A beautiful flower that comes in an array of colours and is incredibly magical with its five petals. It is a great flower for intuition spells.

Waxflower

Chamelaucium

The waxflower is a stunning flower that is native to Australia and ideal for imagination and intuition spells.

Mystical Beings: Angels

One of the main ways the presence of an angel is felt is by suddenly smelling flowers. The smell is of a sweet perfume, such as violet, scented primrose, ylang-ylang, lily of the valley, or lilac. Angels can appear in many different forms, though traditionally people depict them as humanlike with flowing wings. However, they can also appear just as a being of light—a light as bright as the sun, though it does not hurt your eyes to look upon it.

Angels can send us signs that they are around, such as coins, flowers, feathers, and other little things that may be personal to you and that you would recognise, found in unusual places at significant times. That is what I love about angels—the personal touch!

Flower Favourite: Purple Primrose

Primula beesiana

Primroses come in many varieties and are found all over the world. They are known as spring flowers, yet many species now flower throughout the year. The *Primula beesiana* species is a beautiful deep violet colour and one that embodies all the spirituality and psychic powers found in this area of flower magic. Angels are wonderfully spiritual elemental spirits not of earth but of air, and they are one of the highest orders of beings we have contact with, other than the deities themselves.

Angel Primrose Spell

Buy a little primrose plant for the garden or window box. As you plant the primrose, say this spell to ask your angel to be beside you:

> *Angel of the heart, angel of love*
> *Sent by grace from above*
> *Enter my garden and my life*

Help me see wrong from right
Guide me with your trusting ways
Walk beside me please always
Angel of protection, gather your wings
Shield me and all therein
Angel of protection
Shield me under the shadow of your wings

Use this spell to ask for protection and love in all your magical workings. Remember, you always work in the light and in the care of nature. Tenderly care for your purple primrose, and when you smell flowers where there are none, there is an angel nearby.

This final section in the rainbow of flower magic has seen the spiritual and psychic areas prevail. Connections with goddesses and angels run throughout this extraordinarily powerful correspondence. We have also experienced the animal kingdom within this area, and we have come to it via meditation. This is the area where visions and dreams take precedence over the body and mind. It is fitting we end our journey here as we have now reached the highest we can travel to.

Magical Gardens

If you are lucky enough to have a garden, then you might like to try different themes. Just as houses are decorated for a colour or an idea, the garden can be as well. Here are three garden examples with spells for plants that did not feature in the main rainbow chapters. Many of the flowers already mentioned throughout the book can also feature in these gardens as all are magical. Enjoy designing your gardens.

The Night Flower Garden

Many practitioners of the Craft have a night garden that is equal to that of the day. Many witches perform rituals and ceremonies—especially the Esbat, a celebration of a full

moon—during the night hours, and a garden that is in full bloom is ideal.

Further, the plants and flowers we have for a night garden enhance the day garden, too. When dusk falls and darkness creeps throughout the land, while other flowers are closing their leaves, the night garden plants are gently opening to release their intoxicating scents.

The Flowers

These flowers are pure magic. Use these to enhance all your magical practices from spells to rituals to ceremonies.

Angel Wings
Senecio

This amazing plant has beautiful silver-grey leaves that are soft and velvety to the touch. They are particularly striking to plant for a night garden as they seem to illuminate in the light of the moon, but they are equally striking during the day. This plant, believe it or not, is a member of the daisy family and fairs rather well in coastal areas. It grows well in drought areas and does not like wet winter soils; therefore, it makes a perfect conservatory or indoor plant. Its very presence will add protection to any home or garden as well as peace and beauty.

Lamb's Ears
Stachys byzantine

This plant is native to the Middle East, in particular Iran, though it is also found wild in Turkey. Although there is no scent to this plant, its appearance in the night garden is the importance. The plant's tall stems with silver-white leaves give an almost otherworldly quality in the moonlight.

The leaves are soft and thick and densely covered on both sides with silver, spiky hairs reminiscent of the soft ears of lambs, hence the name.

Given its highly sensory nature, lamb's ears is often planted in gardens frequented by children. It is not poisonous, and in some countries it is viewed as an edible herb, such as in Brazil, where it is called lambari. The young leaves can be used in both a salad and a stir-fry. They can also be steamed like spring greens or fried in batter like zucchini or courgette flowers.

Moonflower
Ipomoea alba

These glorious flowers bloom at night and wilt with the first direct sunlight. So, catching them fully illuminated can be tricky. Hence why they are so powerful for magic: rare, white, and they only come out at night, the time of the goddess Diana.

Grow moonflowers in a pot as they can take over the garden. It is also easier for rituals to place the flowers where you want them without picking and destroying them.

Moonflower Night Garden Dedication Ritual

Place your pot of moonflowers in the centre of your garden under direct moonlight. Raise your hands in a *Y* shape toward the moon and say,

> *Blessed be, glory to the moon, glory to Diana*
> *Mother Goddess, watching over all in the night*
> *Sending thoughts of love and light*
> *Your garden blooms of sweet-scented delight*
> *Blessings to you, Mother Goddess*

Thank you for your gifts this night
May you always watch over us with your guiding light

Night-Scented Stock
Matthiola longipetala

This delightful scented plant is native to Europe and Asia. It is so named because it releases a pleasant scent in the evening and throughout the night.

Grow it in containers, borders, and hanging baskets to give a night garden a beautiful aroma.

Stock flowers are also edible and have a spicy taste, much like a radish. They work well in salads. Use as a garnish in a summer soup for added effect. However, do not eat the leaves or roots as they have a bitter taste.

This is a perfect flower for love spells and for use in special occasions, such as weddings and handfastings, births and wiccanings, and communions and awakenings.

Night-Scented Stock Love's Eternal Spell

If a couple has just been married or has moved in together, perform this spell to strengthen their bond. In the night

garden, light two pink tealight candles in front of a photo of each person in the relationship. Have a little vase of night-scented stock on hand. Bring the two photos together and say,

Love eternal, sweet and pure
The love of two bound forevermore

Place the vase on top of the two photos and let the candles burn down or blow out naturally.

Pinks

Dianthus

Pinks are the common name for the dianthus, which also refers to sweet William and carnations. There are over three hundred varieties of dianthus, but the most popular for a night garden is dianthus night star. This plant has tall grey leaves with deep red flowers that have a rich pink margin that seems to glow in the moonlight.

Pinks can be grown anywhere and everywhere, especially in containers, which is handy for night garden rituals and spells as they can be moved anywhere without destroying the plant.

Due to its fleshy hues, pinks embody love, passion, and pleasures of the flesh. Therefore, they are used in many sex magic spells.

In the evening before a romantic night, cut nine night star flowers. As you do, cast this spell. Say it six times.

Love and passion bring this night
Desire in its purest light

Place the cut flowers in a small vase by your bed and enjoy the evening.

The Fairy Garden

If you are lucky enough to have a garden, you might like to use part of it to create a fairy garden. The main plants to grow are lily of the valley and snowdrops, but fairies love the sweet sounds of nature, so make sure bluebells are there, too. Being rather contradictory little beings, they may like a wild garden, but at the same time they love order and will not go anywhere messy. So, an ordered chaos of a garden is perfect for them.

A lawn of forget-me-nots or chamomile and daisies are also good paths for those fairy feet to tread. Rosemary, thyme, lavender, primrose, and winter pansies are great plants to keep in pots; suncatchers and sparkly things, flowers and plants that smell nice, and things that make noise are all ideal in a fairy garden. If toadstools suddenly crop up in your garden, you have fairies there.

If you do not have a garden, just a patio or balcony, use lots of containers to create your garden. Lots of plants do better in their own space anyway, like mint, lemon balm, and sage. As with everything in spirit and magic, work with the environment you have to create what you desire. Even indoors you can grow many herbs and plants; one of the best for fairies is the violet with its small delicate flowers.

Flowers for an All-Year-Round Fairy Garden

When creating a fairy garden, imagine you are making an environment that wildlife will feel at home in. In summer, bees and butterflies will flock to it to feed on all the bounteous nectar; in winter, it will be a place for hedgehogs and ladybirds to nest and huddle down in during frosty morn-

ings and freezing nights. If you can, have a wishing well, no matter how small, in your garden. Fairies love them and use them as portals or magical doors.

Spring

Primrose, daffodil, tulip, crocus, dahlia, geranium, petunia, clematis, wisteria, and bluebell.

Summer

Bluebeard shrub, butterfly bush, smoke bush, foxgloves, oleander, rock rose, potentilla, spirea, rose of Sharon (particularly Minerva), and summer sweet, which has a lovely fragrance.

Hydrangea paniculata can be kept in a container. Carolina allspice is also good, but on no account should you eat it—this is not the cooking allspice. Instead, you can use the seeds for potpourri or grind them up for incense.

Autumn

Aster, helianthus, honeysuckle, penstemon, anemone, dahlia, echinacea, phlox, socks, viola, hollyhock, helenium

(particularly autumn lollipop), poppy (coral reef is especially beautiful), and *Corydalis flexuosa* China blue, which is simply gorgeous—it looks like a fairy waterfall of blue trumpets, and mixed with *Corydalis* canary feathers, it is a beautiful display of colour.

Winter

Winter jasmine, snowdrop, glory-of-the-snow, pasqueflowers, winter squill, the Christmas rose, *Viburnum tinus*.

No fairy garden, or hedgewitch's garden for that matter, would be without winter aconites. They grow in sheltered spots in flower beds and under trees, their small yellow flowers making an appearance in late winter.

Enchanted Garden Friendship Spell

When you have created your garden, no matter how small, enchant it by creating a welcome spell to the fairies. In the evening, place an eggcup of honeyed wine, which is just a tablespoon in a glass of white wine, and a small piece of cake, preferably sliced into tiny squares, in your fairy garden. Recite this spell three times:

In this garden is my home
I welcome all here to roam
From fairies, birds, and bees, please make this home
In the garden and its flowers
You are welcome to spend many hours
To one and all, blessed be

Leave the cake and wine out all night. In the morning, check to see if it's been eaten. If it has been, the fairies have listened, and enjoy their friendship. If it has not disappeared or at least been nibbled at, perform the spell again with fresh honeyed wine and cake.

If you plan it correctly, your fairy garden will be full of life and colour all year round. Remember to leave little gifts out for the fairy folk—even something like a needle and thread, which comes in useful for them. And occasionally treat the wee folk with a little piece of cake, cookies, or even honeyed wine or mead. Enjoy working with the fairies, and they will help look after the garden.

The Witch's Cottage Garden

A witch's typical garden is one that combines herbs with flowers as every plant within the garden will have a purpose. A witch will not plant something just because it looks pretty—all the flowers, herbs, and even trees will have culinary, medicinal, and magical properties. The witch will also be aware of the importance of bringing in nature to the garden, such as insects and especially bees and butterflies and other important pollinators, like those discussed in the chapter Nature's Helpers.

The Flowers

A witch will have herbs in their garden, five of the most popular being sage, rosemary, thyme, mint, and lemon balm. All these herbs flower, and a witch will make good use of those flowers, too, either by drying or freezing them.

To freeze herb flowers, simply wash them and put them in an ice cube tray, add water, and leave them in the freezer. You can keep them as long as you want, and use the ice cube in spells, potions, and rituals as usual.

Lemon Balm
Melissa officinalis

Lemon balm is a relative of the mint family and is a native of Southern Europe and the Mediterranean. It is a beautiful lush green plant with lemon-scented leaves. It has been used in many culinary dishes throughout the world. It is also a highly medicinal plant, with ongoing scientific investigations into its benefits for sleep disorders, depression, and anxiety. Always keep lemon balm in a pot as it can take over a garden—it is as voracious as mint.

Lemon Balm Flower Ice Cube Luck Spell

Light a green candle and create a lemon balm tea. Harvest a few fresh leaves of your lemon balm plant and wash them under running water. Steep them in a teapot with boiling water. Brew for at least five minutes and drop a lemon balm flower ice cube into the cup to not only cool the water but to give an added kick of power. Light the candle and drink the tea. While focusing on the flame and breathing in the silence and calm, say,

Lemon balm, lemon balm
Keep me strong and calm
Bring me lots of luck tonight
In everything I do always make it right

Slowly drink the tea and think about the area in which you need lots of luck. Afterward, extinguish the candle. Every time you need a boost of extra luck, make some lemon balm tea and redo the spell.

Peony
Paeonia

There are many edible flowers that should make it into the witch's garden. One of them is peony. Any variety of peony will suffice in a witch's garden as these come in beautiful shades of pinks, reds, whites, creams, oranges, and yellows. The flowers are edible, and they are ideal in all spells pertaining to the colour correspondences discussed in this book— but they only bloom for a short time.

The other flowers a witch will have are roses, foxgloves, and hollyhocks.

Peony Power Juice

If you are going on a long journey, make sure you have a batch of peony juice on hand to keep you going. Make a peony smoothie using one cup of fresh peony flowers, one small banana, and apple juice or mineral water. Put all ingredients in a blender and mix until smooth. Then pour into a tall glass and drink as you cast this spell:

> *Peony boost*
> *Here in this juice*
> *Power me with riches*
> *The wealth of princes*
> *Wherever I travel, wherever I go*
> *I will have no travelling woes*

As you drink, imagine a golden glow developing from deep within, entirely covering your body. Feel the energy of abundance flowing through you and go about your travels, knowing that whatever you do and wherever you go, abundance energy flows to you, and you are strong and safe.

The other plants the witch will have are belladonna and mandrake—the latter is sometimes called devil's apples due

to its fruit. Mandrake (*Mandragora officinarum*) has lush green leaves and purple-tinged white flowers. It has been used for centuries for a whole range of complaints, including fertility issues and general muscular pain. However, mandrake is highly poisonous, and so it is not recommended.

Another plant the witch will have for boosting magical power is wormwood, otherwise known as silver artemisia.

Silver Artemisia
Artemisia ludoviciana

Silver artemisia is a plant with many names, from white sagebrush to western mugwort to wormwood. It is native to North America. There are many varieties of the plant, and one became synonymous with the popular alcoholic drink absinthe.

Wormwood gets a raw deal and is often frowned upon as being a negative, evil plant. Yet it does have its uses in culinary, medicinal, and magical circles. Therefore, wormwood can be placed in any garden. It is ideal in the night flower garden as it has silvery leaves that shine when the moon beams.

Wormwood is good when used as a resource for banishing, calling spirits, and clairvoyance. It is also good for divination and psychic development and growth. Wormwood is good for spell breaking, but it should be used sparingly in this context. Some practitioners have also used wormwood for love, especially in relation to passion and lust. Remember, wormwood is a very powerful herb and can increase the power and energy of your magical work. It needs to be kept in check as it can be used for aggression, courage, stamina, strength, exorcism, defensive magic, and politics.

Grow wormwood in your garden to enhance the power of all your magical work.

Silver Artemisia Magic Power Increase

If there are spells you are going to do that require extra power, cast this spell on the night of a full moon. This is an ancestral spell, so if you have any photos of passed relatives, take them out and place them near your wormwood or your photo of the plant. Raise your arms to the sky and say,

> *I call forth witches of the past, present, and future*
> *Help me in my path and craft this night*

Increase my power tenfold
But by dawn's early light
Diminish like in days of old

Proceed with your spells for the night. Do not overexert yourself with spell crafting as it takes weeks for you to regain your strength. Until all the spells have played out, keep the photo of your ancestors safe. After, sprinkle salt on it or waft it through incense for a cleanse, then safely store it in your magic box or cupboard.

The Last Word

In this world, we are all connected, and the prettiest correspondences by far are flowers. There is a whole wealth of knowledge concerning flower lore in many hereditary magical practices throughout not only the Celtic world but also the world in general. Flower magic is the purest form of magic, and many practitioners begin to learn the Craft by learning the meaning, name, and purpose of each plant and flower for medicinal, culinary, or purely magical reasons. In hedgewitchery, the mystical beings attached to certain flowers and plants are also learned.

We have journeyed throughout this book learning some of those meanings and practices; it is now up to you to choose what to do with that knowledge. Witchcraft grows

and adapts alongside you as it is part of you. Therefore, choose wisely in your practice, respect the power that you are part of, and always act responsibly with magic, especially with flower magic.

Flowers are a complex contradiction; they are fragile, and yet they are so strong. In many ways, they embody the world we see around us. We may view our world as fragile, but its ability to survive even the harshest of environments and conditions shows that even though things can be dark and bleak, life bursts again and blooms into a rainbow of beauty.

Blessed be and keep safe,
Tudorbeth

Appendix of Flower Spells

Action—Dog Rose

Adaptability—Poor Man's Weatherglass

Animals—Balloon Flower

Beauty—Lady's Mantle

Business—Gladiolus

Career—Ginger, Nasturtium

Charity—Wisteria

Commitment—Wallflowers

Communication—Sunflower

Competitions—Jack-in-the-Pulpit

Compromise—Iris

Concentration—Crocus

Confidence—Snapdragon, Tiger Lily

Creativity—Crown Imperial

Desire—Camellia

Determination—Azalea

Dreams—Heather

Education—Vervain

Enterprise—Daffodils

Enthusiasm—Avens, *Berberis darwinii*

Environment—Zinnia

Envy—Bird's-Foot Trefoil

Exams—Rudbeckia

Expansion—Hydrangea

Family—Love-in-a-Mist

Finance—Cymbidium Orchid

Freedom—Bird of Paradise

Fun—Lantana

Grief—Forget-Me-Nots

Health—Himalayan Blue Poppy

Home—Wolfsbane

Hope—Violet

Imagination—English Lavender

Intuition—Eucalyptus

Joy—Canna, Cosmos

Justice—Blue Wild Indigo

Leadership—Cornflower

Legality—Bluebell

Logic—Viburnum

Love—Dianthus, Geranium, Red Rose

Luck—Primroses

Marriage—Sweet Pea

Memory—Marigold

Mind—Hyssop

New Beginnings—Columbine

Passion—Peony

Peace—Bluestar

Perfection—Lilac

Physical Energy—Poppy

Physical Strength—Chrysanthemum

Power—Cherry

Promotion—Bluebonnets

Prosperity—Glory-of-the-Snow

Psychic—Viola

Reconciliation—Birdbill Dayflower

Secrets—Angel's Trumpet, Nettles

Self-Esteem—Butterfly Weed, Red-Hot Poker

Sexuality—Foxtail Lilies, Trumpet Vine

Spirituality—Passionflower

Strength—Cuckoo's Eye

Study—St. John's Wort

Success—California Poppy, Orange Blossom

Teenagers—Phlox

Transformation—Belladonna

Travel—Lily-of-the-Nile

Trust—Blue Lotus

Vacations—Honeysuckle

Wealth—Christmas Rose

Index of Flower Properties

Here is an A to Z of additional magical plants and their properties. Plant these in your garden, window boxes, or indoor pots to connect to the magic of the universe and our magnificent Earth. These are the magical areas the flowers can be used for.

Aloe—Luck, Protection
Basil—Money, Love
Bay—Success, Dignity
Carnation—Protection, Strength

Chamomile—Passion, Sleep

Clover—Wealth, Success

Dandelion—Divination

Echinacea—Healing

Forget-Me-Not—Healing, Relationships

Foxglove—Passion, Sex

Geranium—Surprises, Meetings, Friendships

Heather—Protection, Luck

Hibiscus—Love, Lust

Honeysuckle—Wealth, Spirit

Iris—Business, Success

Jasmine—Love, Wealth

Kniphofia—Defence, Revenge

Lavender—Peace, Happiness

Lilac—Exorcism

Lily—Healing

Marigold—Career, Success

Myrtle—Fertility

Nasturtiums—Success, Happiness

Orchid—Fertility, Power, Elegance

Poppy—Love, Sleep

Quince—Transformation, Love, Glamour Spells

Rose—Healing, Love, Grief

Spikenard—Protection, Divinity, Angelic Correspondence

Sweet William—Friendship, Love

Tulip—Beauty, Desire, Friendship

Ursinia—Creativity, Magic Enhancement

Vervain—Protection from Negative Energies and Elementals

Violet—Independence, Peace

Wild Rose—Healing, Magic, Prophetic Dreams

Wisteria—Scrying, Seeing Beyond the Veil

Xanthoceras (Yellowhorn)—Success, Victory

Yarrow—Healing, Visionary Arts

Zephyranthes (Rain Lily)—Forgiveness, Peace, Remembrance

References

Binney, Ruth. *Wise Words & Country Ways: Weather Lore.* Devon, UK: David & Charles, 2010.

Coredon, Christopher. *A Dictionary of Medieval Terms and Phrases.* Woodbridge, UK: D. S. Brewer Publishers, 2007.

Crisp, Frank. *Medieval Garden.* New York: Hacker Art Books, 1979.

Day, Brian. *A Chronicle of Folk Customs.* London: Octopus Publishing Group, 1998.

Eason, Cassandra. *The New Crystal Bible.* London: Carlton Books, 2010.

Forty, Jo. *Classic Mythology.* London: Grange Books, 1999.

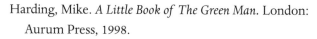

Harding, Mike. *A Little Book of The Green Man.* London: Aurum Press, 1998.

Hedley, Christopher, and Non Shaw. *Herbal Remedies: A Practical Beginner's Guide to Making Effective Remedies in the Kitchen.* Bath, UK: Parragon Book Service, 1996.

Houdret, Jessica. *A Visual Dictionary of Herbs: A Comprehensive Botanical A-Z Reference to Herbs.* London: Anness Publishing, 2000.

Leland, C. G. *Aradia: Gospel of the Witches.* London: David Butt, 1899.

Mathews, John. *The Quest for the Green Man.* Wheaton, IL: Quest Books, 2001.

Michael, Pamela. *Edible Wild Plants and Herbs.* Oxford, UK: Ernest Benn, 1980.

Moorey, Teresa. *The Fairy Bible.* London: Octopus Publishing Group, 2008.

O'Rush, Claire. *The Enchanted Garden.* London: Random House, 2000.

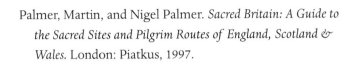

Palmer, Martin, and Nigel Palmer. *Sacred Britain: A Guide to the Sacred Sites and Pilgrim Routes of England, Scotland & Wales.* London: Piatkus, 1997.

Radin Dean. *Real Magic: Ancient Wisdom, Modern Science, and a Guide to the Secret Power of the Universe.* Listening Library, 2018.

Tudorbeth. *The Hedgewitch's Little Book of Seasonal Magic.* Woodbury, MN: Llewellyn Publications, 2022.

———. *The Hedgewitch's Little Book of Spells, Charms & Brews.* Woodbury, MN: Llewellyn Publications, 2021.

TO WRITE TO THE AUTHOR

If you wish to contact the author or would like more information about this book, please write to the author in care of Llewellyn Worldwide Ltd. and we will forward your request. Both the author and the publisher appreciate hearing from you and learning of your enjoyment of this book and how it has helped you. Llewellyn Worldwide Ltd. cannot guarantee that every letter written to the author can be answered, but all will be forwarded. Please write to:

Tudorbeth
℅ Llewellyn Worldwide
2143 Wooddale Drive
Woodbury, MN 55125-2989

Please enclose a self-addressed stamped envelope for reply,
or $1.00 to cover costs. If outside the U.S.A., enclose
an international postal reply coupon.

Many of Llewellyn's authors have websites with additional information and resources.
For more information,
please visit our website at http://www.llewellyn.com.